Improve Your Project Management

Phil Baguley

Contents

Only got a minute?

Before you go any further with this book there's a very simple question that you need to ask yourself – and here it is:

> Why do I want to be a project manager?

Getting an answer to this isn't just important – it's vital. After all, if you've never heard of project management and aren't likely to use it, then why buy the book? But if you have heard about it – and want to know more – then this is definitely the book for you.

But before you go much further there's also something that you need to get clear about. This is that being a project manager doesn't mean that you become a Harry Potter-like witch or wizard. You won't be able to create something out of nothing and you certainly won't have a magic wand that can turn chaos into order.

So what will you be able to do?

The first part of the answer is that you'll have to work hard. Managing a project isn't an easy thing to do. Nor, as you will see later in this book, is it a task for the faint hearted. But managing a project – and doing it well – is worthwhile. For it's a satisfying and rewarding task that's also interesting and challenging. It'll enable you to develop and use skills that are transferable – skills that you can use to good effect elsewhere in your life and career.

The second part of the answer to the question has several 'strings to its bow'. The first of these is that no two projects are ever the same – so, as a result, you're going to find that variety will be the spice of your project management life. The second is that projects are, above all, about people. So managing a project means that you're going to learn how to lead a team, motivate and communicate with all the people involved in the project, and negotiate with them to generate effective solutions to all of the many conflicts and problems that will arise during your project.

By the time you get to the end of this book, you'll have much better understanding of the how, why, and when of all of this and the many other tasks that you'll need to do when you successfully plan, manage and control your projects. By then – if not before – you should be ready to begin, with confidence, the process of becoming a project manager.

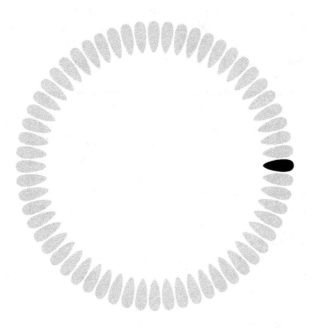

5 Only got five minutes?

Read about a project in your newspaper or see pictures of it on your television screen and you'll usually find that it's one of those multi-billion dollar or pound, decade-long mega-projects. But for most project managers, these are the never-to-be-experienced rarities of the project world. Yet the world is full of projects. Every working day, millions and millions of projects with much smaller outcomes, much more modest costs and shorter durations emerge, are planned, take place and are successfully completed.

These are the small projects of the project management world.

They will appear in your workplace (when you create a performance or quality improvement project) and in your home (when you plan your holiday or remodel or redecorate your kitchen). They are the small projects that you, as business professionals, managers or homeowners, are frequently involved in – often on a part-time basis. Some estimates go as far as putting the total world spend on these small projects at between *50 and 100 times* the total spend on the mega projects of the world. By sheer weight of numbers, these small projects are *the* significant majority of our projects, and they crop up in almost every aspect of your or other people's lives.

Let's look at some examples.

_____

Solar Mali

The people who live in many rural villages in Mali often lack utilities such as electricity or piped water. Getting water and firewood involves the women rising at or before dawn and walking several kilometres in order to gather firewood and draw buckets of contaminated surface water. The children of these villages do go to school, but their schoolwork often gets neglected because of the need to complete chores while there's still daylight.

A non-profit-making NGO – called Practical Small Projects – started a project to educate a village community about solar energy, so that local people could design, fabricate and install a photovoltaic (PV) solar system in the village. Meetings were held with the villagers to determine the best use for the solar energy, and this resulted in a decision to use it to power the local school and a pump for a well. Fifteen villagers were trained as solar technicians – a process that gave them the skills to build, use, install and maintain 35-watt solar modules and a solar pump. These villagers then built the first solar panel ever to be constructed in Mali. The school now has lights, and the schoolchildren now have clean water for drinking.

As a result the numbers of students passing the national examination at the school rose from 6 out of 37 students to 36 out of the 37. The solar-powered electric lights had allowed the children to study in the evenings, after the chores were finished.

Doing up the kitchen

If you're going to sell your house, it's a good idea to spruce up your kitchen. There are three ways that you can do this:

1 *Replace the cabinets*
2 *Get a professional to reface the cabinets*
3 *Repaint the cabinet doors and replace the handles yourself.*

Alternatives 1 and 2 are expensive and could take quite a time, while alternative 3 will be inexpensive and will only take about two-to-three days. So here is an outline of what's involved your kitchen cabinet project:

1 *Remove all the doors and take off the handles.*
2 *Clean the doors thoroughly, initially using paint thinner and then using a 50:50 mix of household ammonia and water, followed by a rinse with clean water. Allow the doors to dry completely. While that's happening, clean down the body of the cabinets.*
3 *If required, sand down the doors and then coat with a primer/ sealer. Note: If your units are polyurethane coated, this needs to be a paint that will adhere to that coating – talk to your do-it-yourself store about which paint to use. Allow the primer to dry.*
4 *Coat the doors with finish paint – two coats may be needed.*
5 *Attach the new handles and re-hang the doors.*

All of this should give you a kitchen that looks bright and cared for – and that will help you to sell your house.

_____

Re-organizing the office

You've decided to reorganize the office. The desks are all in the wrong places, there are phone or power cables all over the place and the overhead lights are always on. Your team isn't working well and something needs to be done!

So here are the steps you need to follow:

1 *Talk to your boss: get his or her support and find out what the budgetary restraints are*
2 *Talk to your team – the people who work in the office – and tell them about what can and can't be done*
3 *Get your team to come up with ideas for the new layout*
4 *Get some costs for these ideas*
5 *Make sure your boss knows what's happening*

6 *Get a consensus agreement on the new layout*

7 *Plan, plan and plan the implementation, and make sure that the team, your boss and your office neighbours know what's going to happen*

8 *Do it*

9 *Review what happened – what went wrong and what went right*

10 *Is it working? Check it out with your team.*

Project similarities

When you think about the what, how and when of these three very different projects you'll soon see similarities. All of these projects:

▸ *had a defined outcome or deliverable*
▸ *had stages in which very different activities took place*
▸ *proceeded in a planned and orderly manner*
▸ *involved uncertainty – because they might not have worked*
▸ *required effective communication between people with different interests if they were going to succeed.*

They also gave rise to outcomes that lay beyond the scope of the initial project. The Mali project, for example, led to better education and examination results – because of the project's targeted outcome of educating a village community about solar energy succeeded. The kitchen project also had a secondary or consequential outcome – the sale of the house – and the chances of achieving this were increased because the kitchen looked bright and attractive.

But that's not all that these typical small projects had in common. For example, the 'doing' parts were all:

▸ *chosen from a number of alternatives*
▸ *organized*
▸ *planned*
▸ *managed in ways that involved the same basic principles and procedures.*

These are often called project management 'best practices', and you'll learn more about them in later sections and chapters of this book. These 'best practices' are, of course, just as applicable to 'mega-projects' as they are to your small projects. As such, they are often seen to generate vast quantities of project documentation. Doing this isn't practical, desirable or relevant on small projects. As a project manager, you should make sure that you only use practices and procedures that focus on and support the achievement of the project's outcome. Avoiding this 'paper-trap' is a key skill when it comes to managing a small project

Nevertheless, when it comes to basics, you should manage a small project with the same level of professionalism and integrity that you use when you manage a medium or large project. There is no room in any project for 'back-of-the-envelope guesstimates' or 'making-it-up-as-you-go along' planning. In other words, as you'll see later in this book, there is no room for amateurism, sloppiness or incompetence in small project management.

Introduction

I'll never forget what the manager of my first project said to me.

'Projects' he said, 'are a bit like Marmite – you either love 'em or you hate 'em.' You can substitute Vegemite for Marmite if you're Australian – but the principle (or effect) is just the same. So, as I loved Marmite, I gave projects and project management a go and, as a result, found that being involved in, creating and managing projects became an important part of my life. The result has been a string of projects that's far too long to be listed here. It ranged (and still does) from small projects at home – such as redecorating the hall or front bedroom – to bigger projects outside home – such as planning and walking the Hadrian's Wall National Trail in Northern England – to even larger projects at work – such as a major rebuild of a chemical plant, the introduction of a quality management system and the reduction of energy usage in a large paper mill.

In each of these projects I learnt something new – if only how not to do it next time. But in each of them I was also reminded of the contribution that working together in a team can make to a project.

So when the idea of writing a book on project management for the *Teach Yourself* series came up, I soon realized that it, too, was a project. However, as I soon discovered, this was to be a project with a difference. For writing a book is something that you can only do on your own – just as you, the reader, can only read the final outcome, the printed book, on your own. But, bridging that gap between the written manuscript and the printed book and then getting that book on the shelves or website of your favourite bookseller takes considerable team effort.

As a result, there are quite a lot of people who have contributed to this project – the 4th edition of this book, now titled *Improve Your Project Management*. These include a good number of the people that I've worked with in the past. They've imparted their influences and wisdoms, large or small, at various times and in their own individual ways. Special mention must be made, however, of two people at Hodder: Alison Frecknall – who joined the 'project' with the previous edition and Jill Birch – who always seems to be there. Their contribution to this – the project that leads to this new edition – has been significant. Mention must also be made of the continuingly wonderful computers and operating system that Apple created, both of which have made the process of transferring thought to text considerably easier than could have been. Last, but by no means least, acknowledgement is willingly made of the considerable help, counsel and support given by my partner, Linda Baguley.

By the way, I still like Marmite.

1

··

Projects, projects and projects

In this chapter you will learn:
- *About the what, why, where, when and how of projects*
- *What the Five Fundamentals of a project are*
- *How the Three Dimensions define its boundaries*
- *How the patterns of its life cycle vary*

Projects old and new

When the Egyptian Pharaoh Cheops died, in 2612 BCE, he was
buried in what we now call the Great Pyramid of Giza. Ranked
for over 43 centuries as the tallest structure on Earth, this huge
edifice is said to have taken over twenty years and almost seven
million person-weeks of effort to complete. The finished structure
contained over two million blocks of stone, each with an average
weight of 2.5 tons. In its original form it rose some 146 metres
above a square base whose sides are exactly aligned to the four
points of the compass and measured almost 230 metres. A massive
project – even by modern day standards – but not the only one in
our history.

The 'top one hundred' list of humankind's projects includes many
other ancient structures such as the Colossus of Rhodes, the
Coliseum of Rome, the Great Wall of China, the Mayan temples
of Central America, the Pharos of Alexandria and the megalithic
stone circle at Stonehenge, England. But the projects that led to
these huge structures were rare, once in a generation, events.

Now, things are different. The project has become an everyday event. It's a regular feature of all our lives and, for many of us, it's a common-place experience to be involved in a project, either at work or at home. So why has this happened?

_____

Projects now

Projects are about change. Without exception, they alter, modify, even transform the world in which we live. To do that they act in ways that are creative, energetic and active. The attraction of the project as a change-creating mechanism is both considerable and obvious. But this only goes part way to telling us why our use of the project has changed – why it has become a part of our everyday lives.

Insight

It's worth asking yourself, at least once a week, a question that goes something like this: 'Which of my current tasks would be completed more efficiently if I treated it as a project?' Write the answer down, keep it safe and – if the same task comes up again next week – convert it into a project.

The other part of the answer lies in the fact that we have all become more aware of the power of the project. For not only does the project create things, it also enables us to use our resources more efficiently and effectively. Today's business professional uses it to plan, direct and execute the ways in which organizational resources are used. In our homes we can use the project to enhance the quality of our lives. As a result, the project has become a major contributor to survival and growth in all organizations, whatever their aims, products or services might be, and a tool for us all to use to shape our lives.

But this isn't the only reason. For the world has also changed. It is, for better or for worse, different from the one that our grandfathers and fathers lived and worked in. Our projects are larger, more ambitious and far more complex. Boston, USA's Big Dig project which replaced 12 kilometres of city centre highway, China's ambitious 40-year project to connect the Yangtze, Hai, Huai and Yellow Rivers, Greece's 670-kilometre Egnatia Highway, the joint American and Japanese Hayabusa probe to the asteroid Itikawa, the world's biggest hydroelectric river dam, the Three Gorges Dam in China and the worlds tallest hotel, the 321-metre high Burj Al-Arab hotel in Dubai are all examples. Our projects also have shorter life spans. In our market places the tides of change are now global, rather than local or national. What happens in Tokyo on Monday is with us on Tuesday – if not before! This means that customer-led organizations, who need to respond to the desires of their customers, need a mechanism, a process, to enable them to do just that – and quickly.

The project is, without doubt, the answer to that need. It's more efficient than the programme, that sequence of activities with a specific purpose of generating incremental change that is so common in our organizations. The project acts as a lens through which an organization or an individual can focus resources and abilities towards a desired outcome. In short, the project enables the organization to delight its customers and us, as individuals, to achieve our goals.

How and why

At the core of the project lies the act of doing. Projects are about work, actions, building, re-building, achievements, deliverables and outcomes. But to be successful they must be managed with care and forethought – in ways that ensure that all of this 'doing' is carried out efficiently and effectively and focused towards a common endpoint. If we fail to do this then our projects will finish late, generate outcomes that are incomplete or inadequate and do so at costs that exceed our planned expenditure. These sorts of project – the failures of the project world – have ill-defined tasks and deliverables, and inappropriate organizations. They are, as you'll see in Chapter 12, poorly led, with ineffective communication systems and isolated project teams. Their plans are inflexible and inadequate. Successful projects plan and track measurable tasks and goals. They build on success in short-term deliverables to generate further successes in complex long-term outcomes. They look for results now, rather than later. Their problems are detected early; the creativity, commitment and energy of their teams drive their projects to success.

Insight

Project success comes when you achieve measurable goals. Failure happens when you don't have clear-cut identified goals.

To make those things happen in our projects we need a map to help us steer our way, a framework from within which we can view the detail of the following chapters of this book, an image that tells us about the project process. Figure 1.1 answers all these needs.

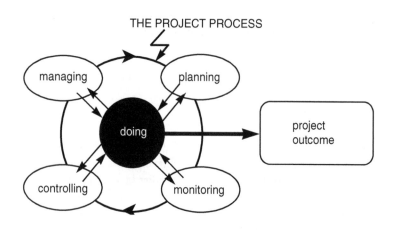

Figure 1.1 The project process.

This not only confirms that the act of doing is core to the project process – it also tells us that it doesn't stand alone. For doing needs to be supported and reinforced by the acts of managing, planning, monitoring and controlling. But all of these need, if they are to be effective, to be carried out within an arena that is built on the foundations of good project management – which is where you come in.

But your involvement has its entry conditions.

There are three criteria that you have to meet if you are going to become an effective, creative, change-generating project manager:

First: You have to need and want to be a project manager.
Second: You must have the opportunity – either at work or at home – to be able to explore being a project manager.
Third: You must have enough knowledge of the what, how, why and when of being a project manager.

The first two of these are down to you. The third one – the knowledge of the what, how, why and when of project management – is what this book is about. But first, before we reach out for that knowledge, what we need to do is to take a good hard look at the project itself.

Big or small

Most people will have heard about at least one big project. The ones that catch the public eye are usually about creating or doing things that are significant, large, expensive and well publicized, like NASA's Mars project, Beijing's 2008 Olympics or Fédération Internationale de Football Association's (FIFA) World Cup.

But not all of our projects are as ambitious or as massive or as costly as these. For every day, all over the world, millions of projects take place. They are launched, planned, monitored and completed with smaller outcomes, much more modest costs and even shorter time scales.

Insight
The total world spend on small projects is estimated to be between 50 and 100 times larger than the total spend on big or mega projects.

New products are being launched, new books published, shops and restaurants 're-imaged' or 'restyled' and old or new businesses moved into new offices. The majority of these have deliverables that are modest, by any standards. For example, beverage vending machines are installed, customer record forms used by Sales Departments are modified, holidays are planned and taken.

If you cast your mind back you can probably remember a similar range of projects – from large to small or modest. It's also worth thinking about the numbers of people involved in those projects and you'll find that these too ranged from those involving many people – as when a company relocates – to those involving as few as two or three in a workplace or a family.

Concrete or ideas

If you ask most people about the projects that they remember, they'll probably tell you about the ones that had performances or outcomes that were tangible. You could see, touch or get hold of them. But these concrete, tangible, outcomes – like a new office block or a new computer – aren't the only sorts of outcome that our projects create.

For our projects can also be aimed towards far less tangible outcomes. These can be, for example, information about customers or changes in the ways in which we think or feel about a particular subject or issue. However, like their cousins with more concrete outcomes, they can still consume huge amounts of money and people time. Some of these are called 'influencing' projects. Examples include car manufacturers' advertising campaigns, aimed at persuading us to buy their newly launched cars; government or federal authority health campaigns, aimed at making us more aware of the risks of smoking or eating too much; and the campaigns of political parties, aimed at persuading us to vote for a particular candidate or party. In our workplaces this sort of 'influencing' project is often about such things as increasing quality, reducing waste or improving customer service. These intangible outcomes are just as important as a new computer or a new office block. They all contain the potential to contribute to the effectiveness and efficiency of our organizations. In our homes these influencing projects can help us to support each other or try to persuade our children to behave better.

Work and play

The projects that you've heard of or worked on so far might lead you to believe that most of our projects are to do with our workplaces. But that isn't so. For the power of the project has spread out beyond the workplace into the rest of our lives. We all have individual projects. They can be about any part of our lives. Some of these are about our home – its size, features or decorations – while others are about our desire to be better swimmers, dancers, runners or golfers. Their outcomes can influence or change things like our own or our children's education, the sort of car we drive, how much we weigh or how we dress. You name it – it is, or has been, somebody's project.

These projects are just as important as our workplace projects. For not only are they statements of our individuality, their outcomes are also often very influential in our lives. They can, for example, result in us changing jobs, moving house, having an extension or sun-deck built, gaining a master's degree, having a holiday in Hawaii, changing or making-over the way we dress or do our hair, or even getting a new partner!

The Five Fundamentals

From what we've seen so far it's beginning to be pretty clear that the project is a versatile and powerful box of tricks.

It can:

- *be about anything that we do or want to do*
- *be large or small – or any size in between*
- *last for decades – or be completed in a day*
- *cost any amount of money – from tens to billions*
- *create things that are either tangible or intangible*
- *involve any number of people – from a single individual to nations.*

And yet, despite this astonishing range of outcomes, sizes, costs and durations, all of these projects have a number of basic characteristics in common.

These, the Five Fundamentals, are present in all our projects:

1 Projects are one-shot events
All projects are one-off events. They come and go, appear and disappear, leaving behind the outcome of our labours. In this, they are very different from the repetitive activities of our day-to-day work. The project's activities begin, the project workload grows from modest beginnings to reach a peak of activity and then the project fades away leaving outcomes that are, as we will soon see, unique.

2 Projects are unique
No two projects are alike. Every project, whatever its outcome, has at its core something that is singular to that particular project. In some projects this singularity or uniqueness is considerable. They have never-to-be-repeated outcomes – like the Pyramids in Egypt or the Thames Flood Barrier in London. In other projects, however, this uniqueness is less obvious and even seems to be

masked by the similarities between it and other projects. For example, a project to build yet another office block in Sydney appears, on the surface, to be the same as all the other office block projects in that city. But it is unique – it has a different design, different contractors, different site, different client, different foundations, different access, and so on.

Insight

If your project outcome isn't unique then you could actually be looking at a 'doesn't-happen-very-often' process rather than a project.

3 Projects have limited and defined time spans

A project is about the creation of something by a specific time. It has a 'deadline' or target completion date. This means that the project doesn't go on for ever. It reaches a point in time when it is complete. When this happens the project is closed, its management team is disbanded and its people move on to other projects or other tasks. The project outcome is handed over to those who are to manage its day-to-day operations. On larger and more complex projects, this time span might cover several years – even decades. It took fourteen years to create the Statue of Liberty! But even these projects reach an end-point.

4 Projects are about change

All projects are about change. They create the new and sometimes knock down the old. These changes can be large or small and can have either trivial or significant implications for our lives. They change the places in which we work and the ways in which we do that work. Managing this change requires special skills. These are skills that are quite different from those needed to maintain the relative stability and predictability of day-to-day operations.

5 Projects have defined outcomes

All projects have well-defined deliverables. These might be a newly built house, a just-published book, a changed business structure, a newly purchased car, or victory in a campaign to be elected to a political office. The pathways to these outcomes consist of linked chains of activities. Each of these might have a sub-goal or sub-outcome, as, for example, when building a house we have to have a sub-goal of completing the foundations. This, as we will see in later chapters, helps the ways in which we plan, control and manage the project. As the project progresses, these sub-goals often become increasingly interdependent. That is, they require other tasks to be completed before they, in their turn, can be completed. For example, in our house project, we have to complete both the foundations and the walls of the house before we can put its roof on. In the end, all of these sub-goals or sub-outcomes must be completed in order to achieve the project's overall goal or outcome.

These Five Fundamentals are present in all projects, whatever their size, cost or duration. Right now you can explore whether you've got them in what you think is or was a project by using the 'Is it a project?' checklist opposite.

Definitions

This is the point in the book at which we need to decide exactly what we mean by a 'project'. In other words, we need to produce a definition of a project.

When it comes to definitions, dictionaries are usually a good place to start. The *Oxford English Dictionary* tells us that a project is 'something projected or proposed for execution; a plan, scheme, purpose; a proposal' – which, as far as it goes, is concise and to the point. But does it go far enough? Does it, for example, tell us about the project's uniqueness, its limited duration or its specified outcome? The answer, of course, is no, it doesn't.

But when we look at the literature of project management we find little improvement. Some writers stress the uncertainty of projects and write about 'risk' and 'steps into the unknown', while others speak eloquently of 'human endeavour', specific

A Checklist

1   Think of a task or job that you currently have in hand or have recently completed.
2   Write down, in a single sentence, what you aim to achieve or achieved by completing that job.
3   Answer the following questions about the job:
   ▷ Did it have a defined start date? Yes ☐ No ☐
   ▷ Did it have a defined end date? Yes ☐ No ☐
   ▷ Did it involve you and other people? Yes ☐ No ☐
   ▷ Did it involve changing something? Yes ☐ No ☐
   ▷ Did it have a clear and well-defined outcome? Yes ☐ No ☐
   ▷ Was the outcome of the task unusual? Yes ☐ No ☐
   ▷ Did the task involve people with a range of different skills? Yes ☐ No ☐
4   If the task outcome was unusual was this because:
   ▷ it had not been done before? Yes ☐ No ☐
   ▷ you hadn't done it before? Yes ☐ No ☐
   ▷ it was unique? Yes ☐ No ☐

Key

If you accumulate seven or more yes's then you probably had a project.

If you accumulate five or less yes's, you have or had a routine task.

If you accumulate between five and seven yes's then you've probably not defined the job clearly – or had a very unusual routine task.

outcomes or simply beginnings and ends. None of these really captures the essence of a project that, as we saw earlier, embodies uniqueness and definitive statements about duration and outcomes.

So, to get out of this log-jam, we'll have to generate our own definition. From this point onwards, this is what we'll mean when we use the word 'project':

> *A project is a sequence of connected events that are conducted over a defined and limited period of time and are targeted towards generating a unique but well defined outcome.*

When we apply this to our earlier examples of projects, we find that they all fit – they all display a degree of uniqueness, consist of activities that are connected to each other and have defined outcomes and limited time spans. This means that we can now begin to view the project as a change-creating mechanism or process – one that we can use to achieve outcomes and create deliverables. We can, for example, use the project at work to introduce a new management information system, change the way we record the details of our customers, restructure our organization, target a new market niche or influence the ways in which our work colleagues think about quality. In our homes we can use the project to restyle our bedrooms, create our sun-decks and plan where we go for our holidays.

But let's not run away with the idea that the project is the only change-creating mechanism that's available to us. Most of us have a whole range of these in our managerial kitbag. However, none of these is as powerful or as effective as the project. The key skill comes in knowing not just when to use the project but also, and perhaps more importantly, how to use it. The next step towards that knowledge comes when we begin to explore the shapes of our projects and in so doing find out more about their boundaries.

The project boundaries

One of the most obvious things about a project is its outcome. Indeed, this is so obvious, that many of us fall into the trap of thinking that it is the only feature of a project. We identify projects by their outcomes, as in London's 2012 Olympics or NASA's Cassini-Huygens mission to Saturn, and forget that all projects have other key and interrelated features.

When we ask questions these features begin to emerge. 'How long did it take?', 'How much did it cost?', 'Was the final outcome as we specified it at the beginning?' and, most importantly, 'Does that outcome do what we wanted it to?' are all questions about the other key features of the project. All of these are equally important; their dimensions define the boundaries of our projects. They also exert a considerable influence upon ways in which we manage them. For example, the question 'How long did it take?' raises the issue of the time span of the overall project or the individual activities that make it up. 'How much did it cost?' draws our attention to the cost of the project. 'Was the outcome as specified at the beginning?' and 'Did the outcome do what we wanted it to?' are both about the project's performance as seen in its outcome.

But none of these features stands alone. They are woven together in a complex web of interrelatedness. As such it is possible to have trade-offs between them, for example, when getting it done quickly costs more, or when adding more features costs more and takes longer. Additionally, the Quality Revolution, with its emphasis on customer satisfaction, means that we now have to be aware of the need to extend our definition of the project's performance to include the quality or 'Fitness for Purpose' of its outcome.

These three features or dimensions – **Time, Cost** and **Performance** – are key to all of our projects.

We need to be aware of them when we define, manage, plan, monitor and control our project. For example, a project to build a sports stadium would be defined in terms of its **Performance** – as in the size of its running track and playing field, the changing facilities, size of car park, etc.; its **Cost** – $30,000,000; and **Time,** i.e. its duration – to be ready for use by 1 December 2015. The quality aspects of this **Performance** relate this project to the needs of the customer and can be expressed in terms of both individual and idiosyncratic factors. These will be objective, such as 'Are there enough parking spaces?' and subjective, such as 'Is the warm-up area big enough?' Think back to when you last bought something major – a house, a car or even an office block – and see if you can recognize the importance of this subjectivity and the ways in which it influences your decisions.

Insight

Fuzzy, ill-defined outcomes, budgets and timescales will only lead to one conclusion – a failed project.

These three dimensions – **Time, Cost** and **Performance** – mark the boundaries of our project (see Figure 1.2). As such they must be clearly and unambiguously defined at the beginning of the project. We must know, for example, how much money we have, when the project must be complete and what the characteristics of its outcome are. These must also be monitored throughout the project's lifetime. If we fail to do this, then we will be unable to either manage or control them and this, without doubt, will lead to failure.

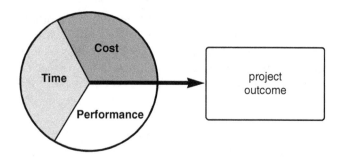

Figure 1.2 The three dimensions – Time, Cost and Performance.

The project life cycle

The idea of the life cycle is a familiar one. We all experience birth, growth, adulthood, old age and death at one time or another. In fact, it's such a basic idea that it's often applied in all sorts of areas. In marketing, for example, it's used to explain the ways in which the sales of a product rise and fall over its lifetime in the market place. In quality assurance, it's used to describe how the reliability of a piece of equipment varies with its age.

So, can we apply it to the project?

Like us, projects have beginnings and ends. They also have periods of growth – phases in which their consumption of money and other resources rises. These are followed by periods of stability and then decline, in which the consumption of resources also changes. Activity rates expand from small beginnings to reach maturity and then diminish and ultimately fall away. In the simplest version of the project life cycle, these are called the **Beginning**, the **Intermediate** and the **Final** phases. But these names don't tell us very much. They don't, for example, tell us what goes on in those phases or what their outcomes are. When we look at the human life cycle we see that its phases have names which tell us what's happening then, such as childhood, adolescence, adulthood, middle age, old age.

The names that we will use in the project life cycle will do the same:

Feasibility phase – in which the idea of the project is conceived, its broad objectives identified, its feasibility reviewed and its initial estimates of cost, performance and time are generated. By the end of this phase our embryonic project has been compared with other projects or assessed against standards of performance. A 'go/no go' decision will have been made – to implement, or not. A 'go' decision leads on to the next stage of the project life cycle (Figure 1.3), Planning and Design, while a 'no go' decision will lead to the project being put aside, to appear again, perhaps, at the next spending round. A minority of projects pass this stage and Chapter 2 describes how that choice is made.

Planning and Design phase – in which growth – developing the detail of the project and its outcome, deciding who will do what and when – takes place. The cost and time estimates of the project are refined. Decisions are made about who should be awarded the major contracts of the project by the end of this phase. Activity rates in this period are, however, still relatively low.

Production phase – in which most things happen, activity rates reach their peak and most of the planned work takes place. Effective monitoring and control procedures are needed in this phase. They tell the project manager what has or hasn't been done or spent, what ought to have been done or spent and what will need to be done or spent in the time that's left. By the end of this stage the project's outcome is substantially complete and ready to be handed over to those who will use it.

Termination phase – in which the project is audited and reviewed and the project team is broken up.

We can see that the rates at which things are done change throughout this cycle. This leads to differing and varying resource demands. For most projects, the Production phase, with its focus on getting things done, involves the peak level of resource demands.

Project priorities

As a project moves through this life cycle, what is important changes. These changes influence the position of the project relative to its boundaries; boundaries whose dimensions are, as we saw earlier, measured in terms of **Time, Cost** and **Performance**.

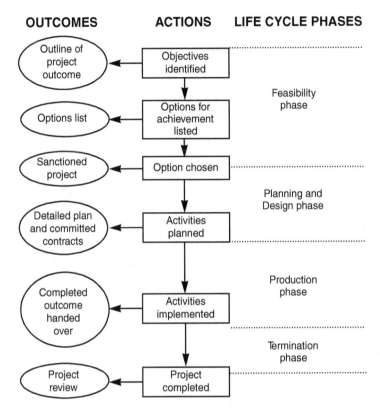

OUTCOMES	ACTIONS	LIFE CYCLE PHASES

Outline of project outcome ← Objectives identified

Options list ← Options for achievement listed

Feasibility phase

Sanctioned project ← Option chosen

Planning and Design phase

Detailed plan and committed contracts ← Activities planned

Production phase

Completed outcome handed over ← Activities implemented

Termination phase

Project review ← Project completed

Figure 1.3 The phases of the project life cycle.

Initially, in the Feasibility phase, these are all of equal ranking and the project is, as it were, equidistant from all three boundaries. As the project survives the rigours of the selection process and moves into the Planning and Design phase, Time becomes more important, taking the lead from Performance and Cost in joint second place. This is not surprising when we realize that most of the initial scheduling and planning decisions are taken during this stage. When we enter the next phase – Production, with its focus on 'getting things done' – the focus of the project shifts initially towards Performance and then, towards the end of this phase, back towards Time. But by the end of this phase the project will have returned to a position that rates Time, Cost and Performance to be of equal importance. This continues through the Termination phase.

Despite these changes in relative importance, all of these aspects are important and none of them should be neglected if you want to achieve the final outcome of a successful project.

Projects and people

In the end, projects are about people. Their creativity, adaptability and energy are needed to plot, plan and manage the project's course. They are involved and interested – as project team members, as clients or as customers, even as the proverbial man or woman on the street – in the project's processes or outcomes. All of these people are, in one way or another, entangled with the project. As such they are project stakeholders.

Insight

Don't forget that, as a project manager, you too are a stakeholder.

To be a project stakeholder you have to have something to gain or lose by the way the project turns out or have an interest, however indirect, in the success or failure of the project. This throws the net in a wide arc. For example, a government-funded project with the outcome of a new hospital will have a list of stakeholders that includes medical and non-medical employees, community doctors, volunteers, suppliers, patients, project team members, local elected representatives, the community, project manager, social services staff, regional health authority, government agencies, contractors and sub-contractors and taxpayers.

It won't take long for you to see that some of these stakeholders have interests that are in opposition. A patient, for example, wants the best possible hospital, irrespective of cost, while a government agency is concerned with issues such as value for money and spend limitation. Nevertheless, all stakeholders are important and finding ways of resolving the conflicts between their often very different needs and demands is one of the major challenges that faces the project manager.

What next?

Now that you know what a project is and isn't about, you can move on to find out about how to choose your project. But, before you do that, read through the following list – this chapter's ten most important messages.

TOP TEN MESSAGES

1 *A project is a way of creating change.*

2 *A project can:*
   ▷ *be large or small*
   ▷ *involve any number of people*
   ▷ *have a life span of days, years or decades*
   ▷ *have outcomes that are tangible or intangible.*

3 *A project has the act of doing at its core.*

4 *This act of doing is supported and reinforced by the acts of:*
   ▷ *managing*
   ▷ *planning*
   ▷ *monitoring*
   ▷ *controlling.*

5 *A project is a one-off event that:*
   ▷ *involves a sequence of connected activities*
   ▷ *takes place over a limited period of time*
   ▷ *is targeted to generate an outcome that is:*
     – *unique, but*
     – *well defined.*

6 *A project's boundaries must be expressed in terms of:*
   ▷ *time*
   ▷ *cost*
   ▷ *performance.*

7 *Each of these must be defined at the beginning of the project and managed and controlled throughout its duration.*

8 *A project's life cycle has the phases of:*
   ▷ *Feasibility*
   ▷ *Planning and Design*
   ▷ *Production*
   ▷ *Termination.*

9 *Each of these phases has its own different:*
   ▷ *activity rate*
   ▷ *resource demands*
   ▷ *outcomes.*

10 *All projects have stakeholders who need to be involved in the project's change process if it is to be successful.*

2

Which project?

In this chapter you will learn:
- *How projects are chosen*
- *About factors that influence that choice, such as risk and uncertainty*

Choice

A project, as we saw in the last chapter, is an active agent for change. But the change that the project brings is not an accidental, 'fall of the dice', event. On the contrary, it is the result of a deliberate, pre-determined, sequence of actions. These are a part of a project that has been intentionally chosen, often from a number of alternatives.

This step of choosing which project to implement, or not to implement, is a significant one. For not only can the choice made give life to our embryonic project, the way that it is made can also influence its chances of successful completion. For if our projects are to be successful, then they have to be chosen well. A poorly chosen project is always a candidate for failure, irrespective of how we manage, plan and control it. When you get to Chapter 12 – project success and failure – you'll find that many failed projects were already infected with the seeds of their failure before they left the selection process. If we are to avoid failure for our projects, then we need to choose them with care – with a clear understanding of the risks and uncertainties involved.

However, for most of us, our role in this project selection process is that of suitor rather than judge. In our workplaces we have to present our potential projects to committees of decision-takers or to the company owner or general manager. In our homes we are faced with the demands of others for the time and money needed by our projects. We have to justify the structure and content of our projects; we have to argue for their right to live and grow. To do this effectively we need to understand this process of project selection, a process that is influenced by two factors.

Insight

Ask yourself whether your potential project is in line with the long-term aims and targets of your organization or family.

The first of these reflects the environment in which we live and work. In this, there are, and always will be, alternatives to all of our actions. These sprout like many-headed hydra along the pathways of our lives. The choice of what alternative to follow is one that is often determined by resource demands. Since these resources are often limited, the answers to questions such as 'What will it cost?' or 'How many people does it need?' or 'How much will we save?' are often key to the decisions made about our potential projects.

The second of these factors is about information. We never, ever, have enough of the 'right' information when we need it. Despite our computer systems and databases, it's always yesterday's data. And this brings us face to face with the uncertainties and risks of our projects.

Uncertainty and risk

Uncertainty, and its cousin, risk, will always be with us. There will always be alternatives that we hadn't thought about, events that we hadn't foreseen and information that wasn't available when we needed it. All of these uncertainties create risk.

For example, when we launch a new product we face uncertainty about whether it will sell. We take the risk that the investments that we make to create that product will not pay off. Similarly, when we reorganize our homes we face uncertainty as to whether the revised layout will be as comfortable and as functionally effective as the old one. This means that we put at risk the investment that we make in time, labour and money to achieve that reorganization.

Insight

'In these matters the only certainty is that nothing is certain.' – Pliny the Elder

For many people, uncertainty and risk are negative and anxiety-provoking. Their instincts tell them to delay, to step aside from situations where these abound, to strike out for the high ground of apparent certainty. But, as is so with many things in the field of human endeavour, these things are relative. For what is risk to us can represent opportunity to others and what is threatening and uncertain to some can be challenging to us. When we face up to uncertainty and risk, while others turn away, then we open up an opportunity to gain advantage. Our new product may then be a runaway success or our home layout may be all that we desired it to be.

But these ventures can never be free from risk. What we can do, however, is to reduce or limit the influence that risk exerts on our project. By doing this we not only increase the project's chances of success, we also increase our ability to manage it effectively.

To do this we need to:

▶ *identify the type, level and source of foreseeable risk*
▶ *reduce or eliminate that risk*
▶ *decide whether or not we will accept the remaining risk.*

This three-stage sequence lies at the core of the larger process of project selection.

Identify the risk

Finding out what are the nature, level and source of our project's risks can take time. But it is worth doing.

We can do it by looking at the two Cs – **Cause** and **Consequence**. We can look at the causes of these risks and then at their consequences – as in what might happen and what would then follow if it did happen – or we can look at their consequences and then at their causes – as in what is an undesirable outcome and how might it be caused.

Insight

Never forget that a risk can either an opportunity or a threat.

An example of the first of these, looking first at a cause and then at its consequences, occurs when we ask 'What happens if the bricks (to build our house) aren't delivered on time?' The consequences that would follow are then identified and listed. These could include delay or non-completion both for the overall project and for the individual tasks that are dependent upon a timely delivery of bricks or the timely completion of another task that needed those bricks.

When we look at the second of these types of risk analysis, the one that looks at consequences first and then identifies the possible causes, we might start by asking 'What might cause us to be unable to tile the roof of our house?' We would then go on to list the possible causes: both direct, as when the tiles aren't delivered on time; and indirect, as when the roof timber installation is delayed by bad weather.

Another way of identifying the nature and level of the project's risk is to use a risk matrix as in Figure 2.1.

PROJECT CHANGE PROCESS

		Been done before	Never been done before
P R O J E C T **O U T C O M E**	Been done before	**LOW RISK**	**MEDIUM RISK**
	Never been done before	**MEDIUM RISK**	**HIGH RISK**

Figure 2.1 Project risk matrix.

Risk	Likelihood rating	Impact rating	Likelihood × Impact [Score]	Actions required	Person responsible

Score risk likelihood and impact as follows:

High = 3, Medium = 2, Low = 1

Figure 2.2 Risk analysis log.

What this matrix tells us is that if our project has an outcome that has been successfully achieved in the past, 'Been done before', and that the ways that we intend to use to achieve it are well proven, also 'Been done before', then we have a low risk project. However, if we intend to build our house using new and unproven methods of construction, 'Never been done before', or build a house with a very novel design or use new 'high-tech' materials, also 'Never been done before', then the risk level of the project will rise. We can also record and rank or assess these risks by using a Risk Analysis Log (Figure 2.2).

But it's not enough just to identify the nature, level and source of our project's risks, we need to do something about them.

Reducing the risk

Once we know what are the level and nature of our project's risks, then we need to make a judgement as to whether or not they will happen.

Again we need to look at the two Cs – Cause and Consequence. We can either estimate the likelihood of the cause happening or estimate the likelihood of the consequence occurring once the cause has happened. The easiest ways of doing this involve either comparing them to other similar risks or drawing from our experience of identical or similar risks. For our house-building project, this would tell us that brick deliveries are routine events and, providing sufficient notice is given, the delivery of standard bricks is an event with a low likelihood of failure.

The level and amount of information that we need to make these estimates change with our position in the project choice process. In the earliest part of the Feasibility phase of the project's life cycle, the objectives of the project will be expressed in broad and general terms and a low level of detail will suffice. Later, when comparisons are being made with other projects, a higher level of detail will be needed.

This also changes when we look at both the nature and probability of the risk's potential consequences. For example, the reactor of a town centre nuclear power plant may be likely to explode once in five hundred years. That is, it is a low probability event. But if it does explode it would cause the deaths of several million people. This combination of the probability of a risk occurring and the consequences of its occurrence helps us. It gives us, even if we have to guess the probability, a basis on which we can decide whether or not to attempt to reduce the risk. For example, if either the probability of the risk occurring is high or the consequences of the risk are unacceptable then we have to attempt to reduce them. To do this we will need further data. But it's not just any old data. For the scope and outcomes of this data-gathering need to reflect both the anticipated value of outcomes and the likely quality and accuracy of the information gained.

Once we have generated these estimates then we can use them to help us evaluate our risks.

At this stage – when the choice is about which project to proceed with – this sort of risk evaluation is generally concerned with the more general, broad brush, issues, rather than the fine detail. Questions such as 'Have we done this before?', 'Has this happened before?' or 'Have we done this in this place before?' might be asked to assess the level of risk involved. One of the ways by which these questions can be answered is by small multi-disciplinary study teams whose objectives are to weed out bad or faulty ideas, identify 'dead ends', and produce a clear assessment of risk and benefit together with recommendations about what to do next. Prototypes and trials can also figure in this information gathering process; a prototype being a first attempt to create a key part of the project outcome, while a trial involves exposing the prototype to users. Both of these cost money and take up time, but they can be cheaper in the long run than the failure that might occur if they were not used. For using them provides us with not only more information about the risks of our project but also the information that we need to reduce those risks.

Yes or no

We have identified the source, nature and level of our project risk and done all that we can to reduce it. Now we have to make a decision – about whether or not to proceed with that particular project.

But risk isn't the only factor that influences this decision.

For example, an organization that is unusually profitable may be prepared to spend A\$400,000 on a speculative high-risk project while an organization with much lower profits would not. Similarly, a non profit-making organization will fund projects that contribute to the effectiveness of its use of scarce or expensive resources – such as capital or people – while a profit-making organization will be concerned with only profitability or the change in its competitive position that results from a project.

The amount of capital available for projects can also vary. It can be a fixed amount, with a consequence of intense competition between projects and the implementation of what is termed 'capital rationing', or it can be unlimited, so that all projects whose marginal cost equals their marginal return are funded. In reality, however, we usually need more money than we have. This means that our estimate of the capital needs of our project can be crucially influential in whether or not it is chosen. The accuracy of this estimate varies, as we will see in Chapter 7, according to our position in the project life cycle.

The factors that affect our choice of which project to implement are diverse and various. They include influences such as legislation, interest rates, the actions of competitors, the current industrial relations climate and, most important of all, whether the project has a strong business case that supports the organization's business plan or strategy. Not the least of these influences are the interests and needs of the project stakeholders who, as we saw in Chapter 1, all have something to gain or lose by the way that the decision about their particular project turns out.

Choosing

The decision as to which project to implement is a conscious and formal one. In large organizations it is often taken by a group of senior managers. This decision-taking group is often called a 'capital investment committee', because of its role in controlling and allocating the often limited amount of capital available for projects. In some organizations, however, its title can reflect the outcome of the projects – as in the 'publishing committee' of a book publisher or the 'new products' group of a detergent manufacturer. In smaller organizations the decision to implement or not to implement a project is often taken by individuals, such as the company owner or the organization's general manager. The range and number of alternative projects considered in these smaller companies may be small. In our homes the decision-taking process is less formal, involving some or all of the family group.

Insight
Choice – rather than chance – will determine whether you take the first step on the road to your project's success.

The techniques that are used to help make this decision are both numerical and non-numerical in nature. We can, for example, make our choice on the basis of the time needed to pay back the initial capital investment or by using sophisticated accounting concepts such as Net Present Value (see page 36). We may also use non-numerical techniques that allow us to express our intuition or preferences. These techniques are versatile enough to be used in a wide variety of situations. We can use them, for example, to decide which make and type of washing machine we wish to purchase for our home, which size, type and make of delivery van to purchase for our small business, which research project to invest in or which site on which to locate our new factory.

Under all of these circumstances each of the alternatives will have different costs, benefits and risks. These are rarely known with absolute certainty. This uncertainty and other factors are brought to bear upon our choice of which project to implement and that choice is, as we saw earlier, a key step in the process of managing a successful project.

Choosing without numbers

There will always be situations in which projects arise without enough supporting information. This might happen, for example, when we need to react quickly to circumstances or when the information is just not available or when we don't have time to generate it. When this happens we still need to evaluate the project but, from necessity, can only do so on a subjective rather than an objective basis.

Some examples of when and how this is done follow.

FLOODS, STORMS, HURRICANES AND OTHER CRISES

When our factory, shop, office or home is threatened by an oncoming storm, flood or hurricane or when the freezer breaks down, we need to do something about it. We may, for example, need to buy storm shutters or boards to protect our shop windows, build a protective dyke to divert flood water away from our home or buy a new freezer. In these circumstances a formal project evaluation is not only impractical – it's also irrelevant.

What can help are the answers to simple questions such as 'Is the factory worth protecting, and if so, at what cost?' If the damage does occur then the question changes to 'Is the factory or office worth repairing, and if so, at what cost?' If the answer is no, then we need to create a new project for a replacement facility. If the answer is yes, that is, that we do need to repair the damage in order to stay in business, then the focus of the project's control will be on the required current expenditure rather than on meeting a budget. However, even this expenditure will have its limits, the most obvious being that you wouldn't spend more in repair costs than the value of the shop or factory.

LEGAL NECESSITY

Our governments, state legislatures and federal agencies all generate laws, codes, statutory rules and regulations that tell us what we can and cannot do in our organizations and homes. These are often subject to change or reinterpretation.

As a consequence the ways in which we operate businesses and what we do in our places of work or homes may also have to change. These are mandatory projects – we have little choice about whether we do, or don't, implement them. Again the focus of the management of this type of project is not on estimation of the costs but on the control of the required expenditure. Examples of this sort of project might include the provision of ventilation equipment to limit employees' exposure to fumes, the provision of wrist supports or special keyboards to prevent RSI (Repetitive Strain Injury), the removal of asbestos from our houses or the provision of access for the disabled.

CANTEENS AND CAR PARKS

Some of our projects are about such things as staff canteens, sports facilities or car parking facilities. In our organizations these are called employee welfare projects and they are generally created, sanctioned and implemented as a result of an organization's human resources policy. They rarely, if ever, generate a financial return of any sort and can involve high levels of capital spend. They do, nevertheless, require careful management, monitoring and control.

Insight

It's worth noting that almost all infrastructure projects are
low risk.

SACRED COW PROJECTS

These projects come about because of the power and influence
of senior managers or senior members of the family. In our
organizations they can have beginnings that are as modest as
the CEO (Chief Executive Officer) asking 'Why don't we have a
look at …', or beginnings which are as complex as an individual
manager's need to prove his or her suitability for a more senior
role by his or her patronage of projects that have a rapid effect
on annual profit. Their selection can often be surrounded with
'political' intrigue and might even bypass the formal project
selection procedures. The best of them, however, may reflect
the intuition or 'gut feel' of experienced, capable and powerful
managers. In our families, their roots are, if anything, even more
complex.

COMPETITIVE ADVANTAGE

In today's fiercely competitive and often volatile business
environment, competitive advantage can make a significant
contribution to an organization's profitability. When a project
is seen to have this potential it needs to be sanctioned quickly so
that it enters the marketplace ahead of any rival and, if successful,
maximizes the profit generated. These 'fast-track' projects are
not without their risks – risks that could be reduced by feasibility
studies or prototyping. Nevertheless, once sanctioned, they do need
careful management and control.

RANKING

Comparative ranking is a technique that is often used to help us
choose between a number of similar projects. Often used when we
have limited or no quantitative information about these projects,
it relies on our ranking them, relative to each other, under a

number of headings. The project with the best total ranking is then chosen for implementation. The headings chosen must be equally applicable to all the projects but will, of course, reflect the nature of these projects. For example, a comparison between different sites for a new factory will have headings that include road and rail access, labour availability, ease of construction and availability of utilities; while a comparison between the different sorts of passenger car might use factors such as capital cost, maintenance cost, insurance cost, ease of parking, load-bearing capacity, ease of passenger entry and exit and fuel costs. A ranking matrix can be used to compare these alternative projects. A matrix generated to compare three alternatives would rank each of them against the others and award each a rating – in this case 1 being the best and 3 being the worst. The overall best of these alternatives will then have the lowest total score.

The advantages of this sort of process include its speed and ease of application and its need for 'better or worse than' assessments rather than absolute numbers.

'NICE TO DO' PROJECTS

These are the 'spur of the moment' holidays, the unplanned weekends in New York, Sydney or Las Vegas or the impromptu shopping trips on London's Oxford Street. These are often unplanned and spontaneous and as such not subject to any comparison with alternatives. We undertake these projects because they are simply 'nice to do'. They rarely generate any financial return and can involve high levels of spend. They do, nevertheless, require careful management to maximize the pleasure and enjoyment that we gain from them.

Choosing by numbers

Money is a scarce commodity and this, together with the complexity and size of the costs, consequences, risks and potential profits of many of our projects, means that we often evaluate these projects by using numbers.

Examples of how this can be done follow.

PAYBACK PERIOD METHOD

The payback period for a project is the period of time that it takes for the project outcome to repay its initial capital investment. For example, a project which cost 100,000 Rand to implement may have an annual profit of 25,000 Rand. The payback period for this project is:

$$\text{Payback period} = \frac{100,000}{25,000} = 4 \text{ years}$$

The project with the shortest payback period is the one that gets chosen. Payback period is a simple and easy-to-use method which is appropriate for low-cost projects. When we apply it to high-cost or long-time-span projects we do come up against some of its limitations – like the fact that it assumes that cash flows after the payback period are of no interest or that money doesn't change in value as time passes.

RATE OF RETURN METHOD

This method looks at the rate of return that the project outcome generates from the capital invested in it. The project with the highest rate of return is the one that is chosen. The rate of return, which is usually expressed as a percentage figure, is found by dividing the annual profit by the implementation cost.

In our earlier example the rate of return is:

$$\frac{\text{Annual profit}}{\text{Implementation cost}} \times 100 = \frac{25,000}{100,000} \times 100 = 25\%$$

This is a simple and easy-to-use method. It is best applied to low-cost, short-time-scale projects, and generates an average rate of return for the period considered. It suffers from its assumption that the value of money doesn't change with time.

NET PRESENT VALUE (NPV) OR DISCOUNTED CASH FLOW (DCF) METHOD

Discounting is a way of determining today's value for money that will be earned in the future. It is the opposite of compounding which tells us the future value of today's cash flows. When we use discounting in our project selection process it enables us to ignore factors like the changing values of the project's goods and equipment. DCF or NPV allows for the fact that the value of money does change with time by converting all of the future earnings of a project to their present-day value.

It does this by using this equation:

$$\text{Net Present Value} = \left[\text{Total of } \frac{\text{Future value cash flow}}{(1 + \text{interest rate})^n} \right] - \text{Capital invested}$$

where: – n is the number of years
– values of $1/(1+\text{interest rate})^n$ can be found in books of discounting tables.

This means that for a project with an assumed interest rate of 10%, an implementation cost of $4,000 and projected profit pattern of:

Year number	1	2	3	4
Annual Profit ($)	1,200	1,500	1,400	1,600

we can calculate its net present value like this:

Year number	1	2	3	4
Value of $1/(1+r)^n$	0.9091	0.8264	0.7513	0.6830
Annual Profit ($)	1,200	1,500	1,400	1,600
Present Value of Annual Profit ($)	1,091	1,240	1,052	1,093

This gives us a total present value of Annual Profits of $4,476. This exceeds the implementation cost of $4,000 by $476. When this happens the project is acceptable because the value of the organization will increase. The greater the increase, the more worthwhile is the project. If the reverse is true and the value of the sum of these discounted future cash flows or present values of future annual profits is less than the implementation cost then the project should be rejected, as the value of the organization will fall.

PROFITABILITY INDEX

The Profitability Index – sometimes called the Benefit-Cost Ratio – is the ratio of the sum of the net present values to the capital required for implementation. If the value of this ratio exceeds 1.0 then the project is acceptable. The higher the value is, the more acceptable the project is. In the example given above the Profitability Index would have been $4,476/$4,000 or 1.119.

INTERNAL RATE OF RETURN

This method of assessing projects discounts the future annual profits of the project over a range of interest rates and then calculates the NPV (for a given period of time) for each of those rates. As the interest rate rises, the NPV falls. The interest rate at which the NPV becomes zero is called the Internal Rate of Return (see Figure 2.3). The higher the interest rate is, the better the project. The choice of whether to implement a project is based on whether this Internal Rate of Return exceeds the cost to the organization of borrowing capital. If it does then the project is acceptable. If it is below this borrowing cost, then the project will be rejected.

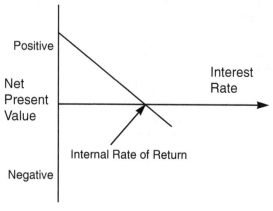

Figure 2.3 Internal Rate of Return.

What next?

In the next chapter you'll find out about how you can organize your project. But, before you do that, read through the following list – this chapter's ten most important messages.

TOP TEN MESSAGES

1 *All projects involve risk and uncertainty.*

2 *Choosing a successful project means being able to identify the risks involved in that project.*

3 *You also need to identify the two Cs – causes and consequences – of those risks.*

4 *Success will follow if you identify the steps needed to reduce that risk and then take a rational, measured, decision whether or not to accept it.*

5 *Some projects will arise because you need to react quickly to circumstances or when you don't have time to generate enough supporting information.*

6 *Projects like these are often responses to*
  ▷ *the demands of a crisis*
  ▷ *the demands of legal requirements*
  ▷ *employee welfare needs*
  ▷ *an individual's power or status needs*
  ▷ *your organization's immediate competitive needs.*

7 *Some projects can just be 'nice to do' – such as a holiday.*

8 *The majority of projects are chosen by using numerical techniques.*

9 *The simplest of these techniques are:*
  ▷ *relative ranking*
  ▷ *payback period.*

10 *The more sophisticated numerical techniques for choosing a project involve:*
  ▷ *Rate of Return*
  ▷ *Net Present Value*
  ▷ *Profitability Index*
  ▷ *Internal Rate of Return.*

3

....

Your project organization

In this chapter you will learn:
- *How to organize a project*
- *About the need for project documentation*

Organizing

Organizing is something that we all do, or try to do, quite often. We organize our holidays, we organize our homes, we organize our days out and we organize our offices. The act of organizing seems woven into the warp and weft of our lives.

So what is it and what do we hope to achieve by doing it?

Put simply, when we organize things we systematize them. We bring things, that were separate, together in ways that are orderly and systematic. When we do this we create a new whole with structure. For example, when we organize a children's birthday party, the things that we bring together are food, drinks, presents and guests. The whole that we create – the party – has a structure, with times and places for playing games, blowing out the candles on the birthday cake, eating jelly, opening presents, etc. The food, drinks, presents and guests all act together to create the outcome we desire – a happy and memorable social occasion that celebrates a child's birthday.

When we organize a project the things that we bring together are:

▶ information – *about the project's outcome, nature, duration, cost, quality and client*

- **people** – *with their skills, creativity, needs, experience and abilities*
- **resources** – *such as materials, equipment, money and time.*

The whole, within which these can act together to create the desired outcome, is our project organization.

But not all the things that we organize are as short-lived or as modest as a birthday party. Some last for decades and involve throngs of people. They provide the connections and co-ordination that are necessary for many of the functions of our society. Their value is such that they achieve virtual permanence as the cornerstones of our societies. These, our organizations, appear everywhere and get involved in everything. They are the dominant forms of our society.

Organizations

Organizations embrace every aspect of our lives. They educate our children, collect our rubbish, sell us goods or services, govern our communities and countries, fight our wars for us and provide us with jobs. Most of us spend the greater part of our lives working in organizations of one sort or another. All the groups, clubs, establishments or societies in which we work and play are organizations. Indeed, some sociologists go as far as to tell us that the family is an organization.

These organizations vary enormously in both size and complexity. They can be small, consisting of limited numbers of people with a common interest, such as playing golf or chess, or they can be huge, complex and powerful, as with the agencies and ministries of our governments or the conglomerates that provide so many of the goods and services that we consume. All of these have ambitions, goals or objectives and they all husband and use scarce resources towards the end of achieving them.

Given all of this, it is not surprising to find that the relationship between the project and the organization is an important one. Organizations, in one form or another, supply the equipment and materials that the project uses, they fund its activities, they train and educate its people and they represent the interests of the diverse and separate groups of stakeholders who wish to influence the projects outcome. But, most importantly, they are the clients for whom many of our projects are created and managed. Because of this we need, albeit briefly, to take a look at the structure and characteristics of the organization itself.

Structures, leaders and people

The structures of our organizations show considerable variety. They range from being highly ordered, with several levels of power and formally defined roles, to being very fluid, almost organic in form, with very limited formality or hierarchy.

Despite this diversity, all these organizations are made up of individuals. These individuals have chosen to come together because they have a common need, desire, purpose or interest. The resulting organizations are usually arranged in ways that are systematic. The outcomes of this arrangement – which can have both formal and informal aspects – are mainly concerned with the ways in which the organization's resources, such as materials, money, information, etc., are used and the ways in which power and influence are exerted. As a result, our organizations have:

▶ **leaders** – *to act as a focus for our diverse individual interests and efforts*
▶ **structures** – *with roles and responsibilities*

► **procedures** – *which are aimed at ensuring that resources are effectively deployed towards the achievement of the organization's objectives.*

But what about the people of these organizations? Organizations need people. Indeed, organizations are people. People bring organizations to life; they make them work, often despite their considerable complexity. Even if we have the best of leaders, the most refined structures and the best procedures, we still need that other vital ingredient – people. Without people, a leader cannot lead and without people's support and compliance, the structures and procedures of the organization might as well be written in sand.

The survival of an organization depends upon its ability to adapt and change in the face of the winds of change. Projects, as we saw in Chapter 1, can answer that need. But if these are to be successful, if they are to help our organizations to adapt, then they too must be organized and this must be done in ways that are compatible with the structures and systems of those organizations. This isnt always easy to achieve as we will now see.

Projects and organizations – the differences

When we first compare projects and organizations we find that they appear to have much in common. They both, for example, have desired outcomes or objectives and they both have leaders, structures, systems and procedures. However, there are differences – differences that are key to the ways in which the project is organized and managed, and key to the ways in which we make sure that the project and the organization are compatible.

The first of these is about time horizons. We already know from the Five Fundamentals that the project has a defined and limited life span. Its time horizon doesn't extend beyond the point at which its outcome is handed over to its client.

The organization, however, has no such limits. Its ambitions are
long term; they extend over the horizon of the future and are, above
all, about survival and continued existence. In contrast, the project,
despite the often solid and considerable nature of its outcomes,
is ephemeral. It is here for a short while and then gone – like the
dragonfly of summer. Its objectives are time specific: they must be
achieved by a certain date or time, one that is known at its birth.
Once this is achieved then the project will voluntarily terminate.

But that is not the only difference. We also know that the outcome
of each project is unique, singular and one-off. But this isn't true
of the organization. Its outcomes are replicas of an original that
was created at some point in its history. These replicas can be, like
the project's outcomes, tangible or intangible, but they are still
replicas. The organization's prime concern is to ensure that it can
continue to – repeatedly and accurately – produce, generate or
provide these replicas. These may evolve or even change as time
passes but at the core of the organization's *raison d'être* lies its
ability to reproduce them.

This comparison tells us about the fundamental differences
between the project and the organization. It also confirms
the value of the project for managers. For the project is a
mechanism that they can use in their quest for what is, for them,
the Holy Grail – the achievement of the organization's objectives.
Projects can be used to create the changes that ensure the activities
of the organization are carried out in a more efficient and more
effective manner. They can even be used to redirect or even
restructure the organization towards the goal of survival.

But, whatever its use might be, the project organization has to be
compatible with its client. This remains true whether that client is
an individual, a family, a small business or a corporate giant.

What sort of project organization?

How we organize our project is important.

Getting it right means that the management of our project has strong, firm foundations. These are the foundations upon which we can build to create the project and carry out its actions of managing, planning, monitoring and controlling – actions which support and reinforce our projects doing. If we get it wrong, then these actions are uncoordinated and uncooperative. Then our project will not only fail to provide us with the outcomes that we desire, it will also fail to do so within its defined boundaries of cost and time.

The ways in which we organize our project act to provide a co-ordinating framework within which these actions take place, as illustrated in Figure 3.1.

But what we do within the project isn't the only issue that this framework – the project organization – addresses. For, as we

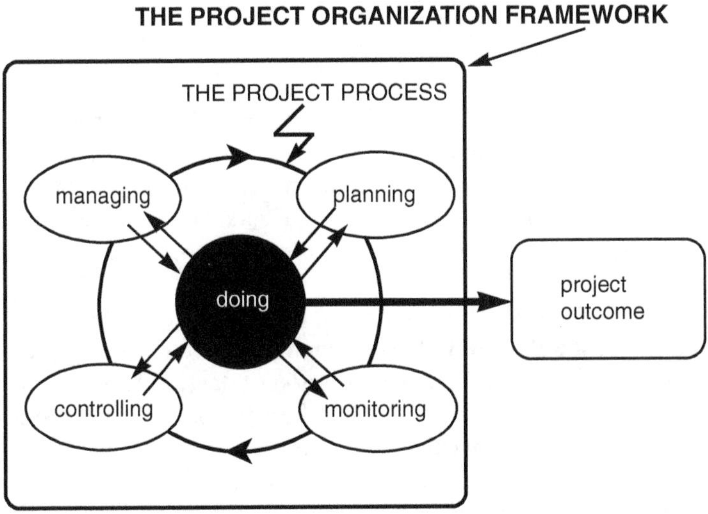

THE PROJECT ORGANIZATION FRAMEWORK

Figure 3.1 The project organization network.

saw earlier in this chapter, the project has to be compatible with the structure, procedures and culture of its client. The key to achieving that compatibility also lies within the way in which the project is organized.

What we can now see is that our project's organization has two faces: that which turns inward – addressing its own internal actions and structure, and that which turns outward towards the outside world – to the project stakeholders, to the client organization. Both of these are important, but each of them must be kept in balance with the other.

For if we create a project organization that is dominated by the project's internal needs then, despite its efficiency, we will find ourselves out of touch with, adrift from, the needs and opinions of the stakeholders of our project. Similarly if we allow those stakeholder needs and opinions to dominate our project organization then we will find ourselves with a project organization that struggles to deliver a project outcome that is on time, to cost and functionally acceptable.

Project aspects

When we make the decision about how to organize our project we must take into account a number of its aspects. The list starts with the obvious – the project's duration – but continues with the project's risk potential, importance to stakeholders, cost and complexity. All of these can influence our decision.

For example, a project for installation of a beverage vending machine has a well proven, low-risk outcome, doesn't involve new technology and has an estimated duration of days. This project will require an organization that is quite different from that of a project for the creation and launching of a manned rocket to Mars, which involves new technologies, a high-risk outcome and extends over a period of years. Similarly, a project with a complex outcome, such as software for a new computer operating system, will need to be organized in ways that are different to the ways in which we organize a project for the purchase and installation of a home computer using Microsoft Windows Vista or Apple Mac OS X version 10.6 software.

Whatever the nature of the project's organization might be, it must, ultimately, enable the project to be managed efficiently and effectively and to be completed to its planned duration, cost and performance.

Project organizations

The spectrum of possible project organizations contains all the possible 'colours' and each of these has relevance for a particular type of project.

To help you choose the 'right' organization for your project we will look, first, at the two extremes of this spectrum and then at a third type of project organization that is often seen as a compromise between these extremes. As we do this we will look at the pros and cons and the demands and benefits of each of these types of project organization.

THE INTEGRATED PROJECT ORGANIZATION

This sort of project organization is a part of the client organization. It is, as far as possible, integrated into the line functions of that organization. The first thing to be decided is under which of these functions or divisions the project organization is to be located. This will depend upon both:

▶ *the nature of the project outcome*
▶ *the nature of the client's organization.*

For example, a project with an outcome of a production facility for a new product would be located in the Production Department while a project that aims to change quality standards and procedures will often, though not always, find a home in the Quality Department.

But what if there is no existing Quality Department or what if the Production Department is organized on a product basis? Where then do we locate our project organization?

The answer can often be a compromise with the project organization reporting to a level of management that is senior enough to make sure that things get done but also has adequate relevant functional expertise.

When you use this sort of organization it means that:

▶ *the project team consists of people who are a part of, employed by, the client organization*
▶ *these people can be used flexibly and in ways that reflect the size and priority of the project and their role in its team*
▶ *the project has easy access to the functional skills and experience of the client organization*
▶ *the same key experts are used by the project and the client organization*
▶ *the project and client organization procedures and systems are compatible, if not identical*
▶ *the project-end shift in ownership and responsibility is smooth and often hassle free*
▶ *the project team members are committed to the client organization and its objectives.*

Insight
When it works, the Integrated project organization delivers measurable value to the client's bottom line while reducing risk.

However, the disadvantages of this type of project organization are that:

▶ *the client organization's priorities will lie with its day-to-day operations and this may limit the availability of key personnel and other project resources*

48

- *on 'influencing' projects, particularly those concerned with attitudes, a project with this sort of organization can be too close to the client organization to effect real change*
- *most project team members will be part-time*
- *the motivation levels of project team members may be influenced by them seeing project duties as unimportant in the context of their individual ambitions and career plans*
- *the responsibility and authority of the project manager can be limited by an inadequate remit, organizational politics or the quality and extent of his or her network connections within the client organization*
- *communications between the project and the client organization can often be informal and unstructured.*

THE STAND ALONE PROJECT ORGANIZATION

This type of project organization stands completely free of and separate from the client organization. This means that it is self-contained and has its own resources, staff, premises, etc. On large projects it can have a structure and systems that are similar to those found in small companies.

When you use this sort of organization it means that:

- *its team almost always consists of full-time members*
- *these team members work directly for the project manager and are committed to the success of the project*
- *communications with the client organization are usually formal, regular and with a senior manager in that organization*
- *the project manager has full control over the project.*

However, its disadvantages are that:

- *duplication of staff roles can occur between projects*
- *project and client organization procedures and systems can be incompatible*
- *the skills developed and experience gained by project team members are lost when the project ends*

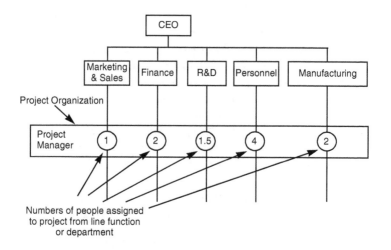

Figure 3.2 *The structure of a Matrix Project Organization.*

▶ *project teams can develop a 'tunnel vision' which ignores the needs and views of stakeholders*

▶ *project team members can be de-motivated by lack of job security or continuity.*

THE MATRIX PROJECT ORGANIZATION

This sort of project organization can be seen as an attempt to combine the good points of both the Stand Alone and the Integrated organizations. Its structure is illustrated in Figure 3.2.

Insight

Working in a Matrix organization can be complicated: you have two bosses, and issues can arise about work priorities, responsibilities and who gives you your annual raise.

It can also exist in a wide range of 'flavours' with the usual variation being the seniority of the line manager to whom the project manager reports. If this is low then the matrix is often described as being 'weak' and the project manager acts more as a co-ordinator than a manager. A minority of the project team members are full-time. In a 'strong' matrix the project manager reports to a senior line manager and acts with more independence and authority. Its team members are almost all full-time.

When you use a Matrix organization it means that:

▶ *the project can access resources, expertise and people from the client organization as and when required*
▶ *the project and client organization procedures and systems are compatible*
▶ *the project manager's authority depends on who she or he reports to*
▶ *the project team consists of people who are employed by the client organization.*

But it has its disadvantages, including:

▶ *project team members have two bosses – a functional boss and a project boss*
▶ *the balance of power, between the client organization and the project manager, can be precarious*
▶ *project shut-downs can be difficult*
▶ *conflict can arise from the fact that the decision-taking of project managers can be limited to administrative decisions while line managers take the technical decisions.*

Your project organization

Before you decide what sort of organization you are going to use for your project, lets review what you already know – or should know – about the project.

It's worth writing this down on a piece of paper. Here are some headings that you can use:

▶ *What is the project's outcome?*
▶ *What is its estimated cost?*

- ▶ *What is its estimated duration?*
- ▶ *Does the project involve new technology or significant risk?*

Now we need to identify some of the detail of your project. Ask yourself:

- ▶ *What tasks are involved in generating that outcome?*
- ▶ *What functional skills and abilities are required in order to achieve that outcome?*
- ▶ *What equipment is required in order to achieve that outcome?*

Now you need to look at the client organization and ask yourself:

- ▶ *Does it have the functional skills, abilities and equipment that the project requires?*
- ▶ *Will it be able to release them for use on the project?*
- ▶ *Does it have individuals with the project management skills and experience required?*

Finally, ask yourself:

- ▶ *What previous project experience does the client organization have?*
- ▶ *How were these projects organized?*
- ▶ *Which of them were successful?*

By now, you should have all the information that you need to decide what sort of project organization you are going to have.

Here is a check list to start you on your way towards that decision:

Your project organization

Answer the following questions by ticking the 'yes' or the 'no' box. Then add up the number of yes's and no's that you have.

Is your project planned to have a long duration? Yes ☐ No ☐

Is the cost of your project substantial? Yes ☐ No ☐

Does your project involve high levels of risk? Yes ☐ No ☐

Key

Three yes's – use a Stand Alone project organization

Two yes's, one no – choose between a Matrix and a Stand Alone project organization

Two no's, one yes – choose between a Matrix and a Stand Alone project organization

Three no's – use an Integrated project organization

Here, also, are a few pointers that should help you to continue that journey:

1 *Large, long, costly projects usually need either Stand Alone project organization or strong Matrix organization so that the resources they need are available when required.*
2 *If your client organization hasn't got the functional skills and abilities required to achieve the project outcome, or can't release them for the project, then you need a Stand Alone project organization that can effectively control, monitor and manage the subcontractors that you'll need to use.*
3 *If the project involves new technology then your choice of what organization to use must reflect whether your client organization has the feasibility study, prototyping and R&D (research and development) evaluation skills that will be needed. If it has, then use either an Integrated or a strong Matrix organization. If it hasn't, you'll have to subcontract these and will probably need a Matrix or a Stand Alone project organization.*

4 *Small, short, low-cost projects are usually best handled by an Integrated project organization except when the project outcome is very significant to the client organization (see Chapter 11).*

These pointers aren't intended as firm and hard 'golden' rules about the sort of organization that you choose. Your own experience and the experience of your client organization are just as important – as is, of course, your own judgement.

Programme or portfolio?

Using the project to create a specific identified change has become so popular in today's organizations that you'll often find several projects running alongside each other, using shared resources but doing that in different locations and towards different outcomes in a single organization. When this happens life can, and does, get very complicated. Resources get stretched, priorities confused and disorder raises its ugly head. As a result, two techniques have been developed to try and control this sort of situation. Both have project management as a core discipline and both have the objective of relating the groups of projects to the strategic objectives of the organization.

PROJECT PROGRAMME MANAGEMENT

Insight

In its simplest form Programme Management can be described as 'a group of projects managed together for added benefit'.

This gets used when the organization's projects are related, as, for example, in the design, manufacturing and marketing of a new automobile when the project count can reach up into the hundreds or even the thousands. The Project Programme Management technique allows these multiple projects to be run concurrently and enables significant benefits to be generated by treating them as them as a collection. This collection will be focused on ongoing business change and new projects will be added as old ones are completed. The Programme Management technique has objectives that are strategic and long term; it is, as someone once said, about 'a journey rather than a destination'. As such it crosses over the functional boundaries that exist within an organization and needs to be managed at a senior level.

PORTFOLIO MANAGEMENT

Insight

Project Portfolio Management begins when an organization generates a comprehensive list of all its projects and their objectives.

A portfolio, so the dictionary tells us, is 'a range of products, services, assets, or qualities offered or possessed'. In its purest form, Portfolio Management casts its net a lot wider than Project Programme Management. For not only does it embrace all of an organization's projects – related or not – it also embraces its products, services assets, operations resources and people. The objective of this set of business practices and techniques is to make sure that all of these are aligned with the strategic objectives of the organization. Management at a senior level of the organization is a must for this technique – which can also be applied exclusively to an organization's projects.

Project procedures and specifications

Whatever sort of project organization that you end up choosing, you have to make sure that the internal processes of the project are organized and conducted effectively and efficiently. The project will still need to be planned (see Chapter 4), managed (see Chapter 5), have cost estimates and budgets (see Chapter 7) and be monitored and controlled (see Chapter 8).

So that these actions can take place and contribute to the success of the project, we need to use good working practices to run our project. We can find examples of these in the international, national and industry specific standards such as PRINCE (see opposite), PROMPT, RIBA's 'Plan of Work', Australia's HIA Quality Management and Systems, America's standards for Software Project Management (IEEE), Project Management (AIA) and Cost Engineering and Project Management (ANSI) and the British Standards Guide to Project Management (BS6079) and Use of Network Techniques in Project Management (BS6046). Further details of these can be accessed through the American National Standards Institution standards search site (see 'Taking It Further' for web address). You might also find them in the procedures and specifications of your workplace's Manual of Project Organization and Procedures. Its worth getting access to one of these – you may not want to use all of the procedures but they'll give you some useful pointers on how to do it well.

These documents will act as blueprints for the way in which the activities of our project ought to be conducted. As such they are generalized. What we need for our project is documentation that is specific to that project; documentation that tells us what our project is about and how it will be conducted. This is usually called a project manual.

So what do we need in our project manual? The simple answer is that it should contain the information that we, as project managers, need in order to manage the project. This means that, whatever the size, cost or nature of our project, we should have a source of information that tells us clearly and unambiguously about the Cost, Time and Performance aspects of our project and how we are going to manage, monitor and control those aspects. It doesn't have to be a massive tome – as you'll see shortly, it can be a few sheets of paper.

You should seriously consider including the following:

PROJECT SPECIFICATION OR PROJECT INITIATION DOCUMENT (PID)

This is a must for all projects. It tells us what the project's objectives, duration and sanctioned cost are. For a short, low-cost project a single sheet of paper will be sufficient. A complex,

PRINCE is an acronym that stands for Projects In Controlled Environments. It's a management method that covers the management, control and organization of a project. Initially developed in 1989 and used as a UK Government standard for information technology (IT) project management, PRINCE was soon in regular use outside the purely IT environment.

PRINCE2 refers to the second major version of this method and is a registered trademark of the UK Office of Government Commerce (OGC). PRINCE2 was released in 1996 as a generic project management method and is scheduled for review in 2008/09.

PRINCE2 breaks the overall project process down into eight processes that in turn contain a total of 45 separate sub-processes. These processes are:

1 Starting Up a Project (SU)
2 Planning (PL)
3 Initiating a Project (IP)
4 Directing a Project (DP)
5 Controlling a Stage (CS)
6 Managing Product Delivery (MP)
7 Managing Stage Boundaries (SB)
8 Closing a Project (CP).

The PRINCE2 process is described more fully on the website of the UK Government's Office of Government Commerce (www.ogc.gov.uk).

Project Specification Form

Project title: Reference no:

Project objectives:

Project deliverables:

Project manager: Tel no:

Project sponsor: Tel no:

Start date: Completion date:

Capital sanctioned: Estimate ref no:

Project team: Client contacts:

Approved by:
Project manager: Date:

Project sponsor: Date:

Figure 3.3 Sample Project Specification Form.

high-cost or long-duration project will need something more substantial, often a separate volume of the project manual, with sections and appendices containing the detail of the project. This specification will have evolved as the project developed and may have been amended and rewritten several times. But once the project is given the go ahead, this specification should be frozen. From that point onwards, this specification should be subject to very little change or revision and any that does take place should be strictly controlled (see 'Project change control' below). As the definitive source of information about the project, it should contain the project's goals and objectives, scope, organization, budget and justification as well as telling us which techniques and systems we will use to plan, monitor and control the project.

Insight

If you can't fill in every part of your Project Specification Document, then you're not ready to start your project.

Figure 3.3 is a simple version of a Project Specification Form.

PROJECT ROLES AND RESPONSIBILITIES

If our project is big enough to need a project team (see Chapters 6 and 11) then we need to know what the duties and responsibilities of each of the team members are. We also need to know what is expected of us when we carry out a particular role in that team. This information can be provided in the form of:

▶ *job descriptions*
▶ *responsibility charts.*

An effective job description should define:

▶ *what the job should achieve*
▶ *what it needs to do to achieve that*
▶ *to what other position or job it is responsible*

▶ *what authority the job has in terms of decision making, hiring and firing, spending, etc.*

▶ *what responsibility, if any, it has for client communications*

▶ *how its performance is measured.*

Two sides of A4 paper are all you should need for this – any more than that indicates that you're not sure about what you want the job to do for you. If you're not sure about the objectives and responsibilities of the job, how can you expect the job holder to be?

TASK AREA	Project Manager	Mechanical Engineer	Civil Engineer	Electrical Engineer	Instrument Engineer	Process Design Engineer
Flowsheet design	◆	■		■	❖	●
Plant layout	◆	●	❖	■	■	■
Piping design	◆	●	■		❖	■
Instrumentation	◆			■	●	❖
Power supply	◆			●	■	

Key:
- ● Responsible
- ◆ Approval
- ■ Notified
- ❖ Support

Figure 3.4 Sample responsibility chart for an engineering project.

A responsibility chart gives us a bird's eye view of who is responsible for what over the whole project. The level of detail shown should reflect both the size and complexity of the project as well as the needs of the project team. This is illustrated in Figure 3.4.

PROJECT ESTIMATES AND BUDGETS

We look at the estimates and budgets of our project in more detail in Chapter 7. Both of these are important, though their uses are different. It's essential that your project manual identifies exactly what sum of money has been sanctioned and tells you what procedures will be used for expenditure approval and invoice payment and who is responsible for signing cheques, etc.

PROJECT CHANGE CONTROL

Despite the best of intentions, changes do happen, even on projects that are excellently managed. These can range from the substantial, as when new technology becomes available, to the small, as when detailed design work progresses and shows us a better way to do something. They can come about because of changes in legislation, or because of new technology, better designs, etc. They can also come about because of mistakes and errors. Whatever their origin or size might be, all of these changes have the potential to alter the project's duration or cost or the nature and quality of its outcome.

It is essential that these changes are controlled. This means that, at the earliest possible opportunity, an effective change procedure must be established. This will require a clear, accessible and unambiguous statement of the project's 'base' line – as in the project specification mentioned above – and a process for the definition, evaluation and approval of any proposed changes to that specification.

Project Change Request	
Number:	Date:
Approved/Rejected/Held	
Proposed change:	
Reasons for change:	
Areas affected:	
Documents and drawing affected:	
Requested by:	Evaluated by:

Figure 3.5 Sample Project Change Request form.

A typical basic project change control form will contain:

▶ *an outline of proposed change*
▶ *the reasons for the proposed change*
▶ *which areas, costs, documents and drawings of the project are affected*
▶ *who requested the change*
▶ *who evaluated and approved/rejected the change.*

See Figure 3.5 for an example of a simple Project Change Request form.

What next?

Projects need to be planned and in the next chapter you'll take a look at the ways in which you can do that. But, before you do that, read through the following list – this chapter's ten most important messages.

TOP TEN MESSAGES

1 *Projects need to be organized.*

2 *Choosing the sort of organization that your project will use is important.*

3 *That organization needs to be compatible with the client organization.*

4 *It also needs to provide a framework for the project's Doing, Planning, Monitoring and Controlling.*

5 *One alternative for your project organization is the Integrated organization is which, as far as possible, is integrated into the line functions of the client organization.*

6 *Another alternative is the Stand Alone organization which stands completely free of and separate from the client organization, is self-contained and has its own resources, staff, premises, etc.*

7 *Matrix organization is a third and final alternative type of organization for your project that combines the good points of both the Stand Alone and the Integrated organizations.*

8 *To choose the right organization for your project you need to:*
   - ▷ *find out and understand what has worked in the past*
   - ▷ *understand the client organization's skills, experience and equipment*
   - ▷ *be aware of the project's outcomes, risks, costs, duration and special technology or knowledge needs*
   - ▷ *decide what will work for you.*

9 *Then you need to generate:*
   - ▷ *a project specification*
   - ▷ *job descriptions*
   - ▷ *responsibility charts.*

10 *You'll also need procedures for:*
- ▷ *budget control*
- ▷ *accounting*
- ▷ *change control.*

4

Plans for your project

In this chapter you will learn:
- *The value of project planning*
- *About ways to order and sequence a project to maximum effect*
- *About the steps and stages of the planning process and the tools needed*

Planning – now or never

When we look up the word 'plan' in the *Oxford English Dictionary* we are faced with a herd of alternative meanings.

A plan can be, amongst other things, a 'scheme for the economic development of a country', a 'drawing or diagram showing the relative positions of the parts of a building' or even, for John Wesley's early English Methodist Church, a 'periodic document listing the preachers for all the services throughout a circuit for the period'. These and other examples tell us that the plan is a versatile and commonly used commodity. The act of generating one – or planning – is something that many of us do.

That is to say that we all, at some time and in some way, 'devise, contrive, design something to be done, or some action or proceeding to be carried out' (*OED*).

The results of all this planning are, of course, our attempts to control the future. However, things don't always work out in the ways that we intend them to. As a result, we often have to face a reality that is different, in one way or another, to the one that we had planned. As somebody once said, 'The future is not what it was.'

In our workplaces, the plans that we make are often challenged. The need for adaptability, the need to respond to customer needs, the tides of employee empowerment, decentralization, down-sizing and sweeping organizational re-engineering are just some of the things that act against our plans. Indeed, in today's workaday world many of the traditional management wisdoms, for which planning and control were core issues, seem to have been challenged – and overthrown.

But is planning as out-of-date and old-fashioned as it seems – has it really been discarded in favour of today's instant responsiveness aided by ever faster computers? Or is it a powerful and flexible tool whose intelligent use we need to relearn in these volatile days?

The devil, as always, is in the detail and our answer lies not so much in the act of planning, but in the way that we use the plans that planning generates. For these are more than just lists of possible future actions. At their best, they are powerful visions of our hoped-for futures; our claims for immortality. At their worst, however, they are unyielding, intractable expressions of the demands of others that suppress and choke our individual creativity and spontaneity. The difference between these two extremes lies not so much in the plan itself as in the ways in which we use it.

And therein lies the plan's deliverance. For as long as we need to reach out and try to shape and control our futures, then we will need to use the plan to help us achieve that end.

Projects and planning

The project and the plan are long-term bed mates. The project is a consciously chosen event and the plan is integral to its creation and completion. But the plan that we create must be resilient and adaptable if it is to be capable of withstanding the buffets and storms of our increasingly changeable workplaces. To cope it must be able to change – without losing sight of its endpoint, the project's outcome.

Insight
Failing to plan means that you are planning to fail.

The act of planning is, in its essence, about the creation of a plan. That plan can take many forms – it can be a diagram, a table of figures, a programme of dates or a sequence of actions. But, whatever its form, it is a statement of our intentions regarding the future relationships of the times, places, etc. of our intended actions.

Our plan for a holiday might, for example, include the actions of obtaining visas, getting traveller's cheques, arranging for the cats to be fed while we are away, cancelling the deliveries of newspapers and milk and buying guides or maps for the areas in which we are going to travel.

But knowing what we intend to do isn't enough. We also need to know:

▶ *when these actions are going to take place*
▶ *who is going to do them*
▶ *what resources are needed to do them.*

Our holiday plan must tell us to apply, in good time, for our visas, to make sure we've enough money in our bank accounts when we buy our traveller's cheques and to make sure the neighbours or friends who usually feed our cats aren't away at the same time that we intend to be.

The plans of our projects have the same needs. They also need to know the what, when, who and with what of our actions if they are to enable us to shift their outcomes from desire to reality

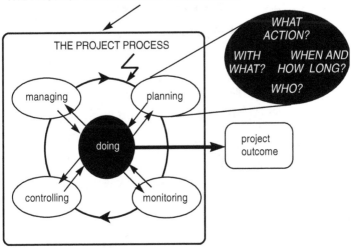

THE PROJECT ORGANIZATION FRAMEWORK

THE PROJECT PROCESS

WHAT ACTION?

WITH WHAT?   WHEN AND HOW LONG?

WHO?

managing

planning

doing

controlling

monitoring

project outcome

Figure 4.1 Planning and the project process.

(see Figure 4.1). If we plan without attention to these details then not only do we limit our ability to create the desired outcome of our project within its specified cost and time limits, we may also limit our ability to create it at all.

Insight

Detailed, systematic, team-involving planning is the single most important thing that project managers do.

The details of these future actions will, of course, be particular to the project that we are planning and are often contained in what is called a Work Breakdown Schedule (WBS – see Chapter 7). A simple example, for a small domestic project that may be familiar to some of you, is given in Figure 4.2.

But the project's outcome, actions and duration aren't the only issues. We mustn't forget that our project has a budgeted cost and that a certain level of quality is implicit in its outcome specification. Both of these could affect either the way that we undertake the

The English Project

Project goals and objectives: To make a cup of tea

Actions needed:
- check kettle water level and adjust as required
- switch on kettle
- get teapot
- get leaf tea
- get milk or slice of lemon
- get cup, saucer and jug
- put milk in jug or lemon on saucer
- allow kettle to boil
- switch off boiling kettle
- warm teapot by rinsing with hot water
- put leaf tea in teapot
- pour hot water into teapot
- leave to brew or infuse
- get strainer
- pour tea through strainer into cup
- add milk or lemon to tea

Duration: maximum of 10 minutes. **Actions by:** Phil Baguley

Equipment, tools and material needed:

Power point	Electric kettle,[1] lead and plug	Tea strainer
Cold water tap	Bottle of milk[2] in a refrigerator	
Teapot	Packet of leaf tea	Cup and saucer
Teaspoon	Jug for milk	

Notes: 1 Kettle suitable for gas stove is acceptable alternative
       2 Slice of lemon is acceptable alternative

Figure 4.2 The English Project – objectives, actions and needs.

required actions or even the actions themselves. For example, in our English Project, the size of our budget will influence what sort of leaf tea we use and might even, if we have a restricted budget, persuade us to use a teabag rather than leaf tea. As a consequence of using this teabag we wouldn't need a teapot or a tea strainer and the sequence of actions that we followed would be different – as would the quality of the resultant tea. In summary, this cost factor can influence:

▶ *the quantity of the project's outcome (a pot of tea or a mug/ cup of tea)*
▶ *the time taken to complete the project (teabag is quicker and less total time needed)*
▶ *outcome quality or fitness for purpose (does tea made from a teabag taste as good as tea made from leaf tea?).*

Interdependency

The actions of a plan are always linked. Some of them, for example, cannot be started until other actions are finished – these are 'interdependent' activities, while other actions can be conducted at the same time – these are 'parallel' activities. When we look at our English Project, we find, for example, that the action of 'switch on kettle' should only take place after we've completed the action of 'check kettle water level and adjust as required'. Similarly the action of 'warm teapot by rinsing with hot water' can only follow the water in the kettle reaching boiling point and the action of 'switch off boiling kettle'.

Insight
'Interdependence: The fact or condition of depending each upon the other; mutual dependence.' (*OED*)

See if you can spot any more of these interdependent relationships, and then compare your answers with those given in Figure 4.3.

These relationships are important. For once we have found them, the detail of the project's plan begins to emerge. We can then begin,

Action number		Must be completed before or after Action number
1	Check kettle water level and adjust as necessary	Before 2
2	Switch on kettle	After 1
3	Get teapot	Before 10
4	Get leaf tea	Before 11
5	Get milk or sliced lemon	Before 7
6	Get cup, saucer and jug	Before 7
7	Put milk in jug or lemon on saucer	Before 16
8	Allow kettle to boil	After 2
9	Switch off boiling kettle	After 8
10	Warm teapot by rinsing with warm water	After 9
11	Put leaf tea in teapot	After 3, 4 & 10
12	Pour hot water into teapot	After 11
13	Leave to brew or infuse	After 12
14	Get strainer	After 12
15	Pour tea through strainer into cup	After 14 &13
16	Add milk or lemon to taste	After 15

Figure 4.3 Action plan for the English Project.

for example, in our English Project, to ask questions like, 'Can we get the teapot, milk and cup and saucer while the kettle is boiling?' or alternatively, 'Can we get the milk and cup and saucer while the tea is infusing?' The answers will make a difference not only to the order in which we carry out our actions but also to the resources that we need to carry them out. But to be sure about that we also need to know how long each of these activities will take.

When we estimate the duration of these activities we can use a number of sources of information. For example, we can use measurements of the times taken for similar actions, we can get advice from others or we can draw on our own experience. For our

English Project we can generate action times by using information from the kettle manufacturers (2 litres of water will boil in three minutes), the people who market the tea (to ensure full infusion use freshly boiled water and leave standing for five minutes), people who have done it before (friends, family or books) and our own experience (what did we do last time?). It's not necessary for these estimates to be absolutely accurate. For example, it will be enough, in our English Project, to be able to say how long the activities will take to within the nearest half minute. Remember that this is an initial estimate and that you'll have the opportunity later to refine this estimate, if you need to. On larger, longer and more complicated projects an accuracy of ± half a day will suffice at this stage in the planning process.

Insight

Keep your plan simple enough to be clear and understandable, but not so simple that it's unrealistic.

Whatever the accuracy of our estimates might be, the resulting plan needs to have certain characteristics. It needs to be clear, unambiguous and easily understood. It needs to contain enough detail to be meaningful and usable, but not so much detail that it becomes unnecessarily complicated. It also needs to be easy to change, update and revise as the timeline of the project progresses, so that we can monitor and record project progress. If our plan has all of these characteristics then it is not only usable, it is also a tool, an enabling mechanism that helps us to meet our goals.

A good plan will have all of these characteristics while a bad plan will be difficult to understand, awkward to use and contain inadequate or irrelevant detail.

Bars and charts

Most information is best presented in a visual form, style or manner and the project plan is no exception.

One of the best and simplest ways of doing this is by the use of the bar chart or Gantt chart. This was developed around 1910 in America by an engineer called Henry L. Gantt. Despite its age, it remains a popular method of presenting information about the project plan. The Gantt chart has a horizontal time scale, a vertical list of activities and a series of horizontal lines or bars with one for each activity. The length of each of these bars is proportional to the time needed to complete the activity that it represents.

A typical Gantt chart for a part of the English Project looks like the one in Figure 4.4. This shows us:

▶ *when activities start and finish*
▶ *whether they have been completed*
▶ *the project status at the point in time at which the chart was prepared*
▶ *which activities are 'parallel' activities and can be done at the same time as others.*

The Gantt chart can also show us the project's 'Critical Path'. This is the sequence, or pathway, of activities that determines the total project duration. If any of the activities on this pathway is delayed or extended then the completion time of the whole project is delayed. This pathway and the activities that make it up tell us which project activities we need to focus on to ensure that the project is completed on time.

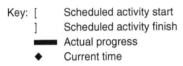

Activity description	Activity number	Minutes						
		1	2	3	4	5	6	7
Check kettle water level and adjust as required	1	[▬▬▬]						
Switch on kettle	2			[ ]				
Get teapot	3			[ ]				
Get leaf tea	4				[ ]			
Get milk or sliced lemon	5				[ ]			

Key: [Scheduled activity start
      ]   Scheduled activity finish
      ▬▬▬   Actual progress
      ◆   Current time

Figure 4.4 A typical Gantt chart.

Both the critical path and the 'same time' or parallel activities
are shown on the full Gantt chart for the English Project (see page
76). When we look at this we can see that the project takes 11½
minutes to complete, compared with a target of 10 minutes, and
that Activity 1 'Check kettle water level and adjust', Activity 2
'Switch on kettle', Activity 8 'Allow kettle to boil' and Activity 13
'Leave to brew or infuse' represent a major part of the Critical
Path. If we were to reduce the kettle boil period by using a more
powerful kettle or less water, then we would reduce the overall
project duration. But this wouldn't be a reduction without limit
as further inspection of the chart shows us that when we reduce
the kettle boiling period from 3 minutes to 2 minutes or less we
change the Critical Path. Activities 3, 4, 5, 6 and 7 then replace
Activity 8 on this path. However, the sequence of Activities 5, 6
and 7 – which are about getting the milk or lemon ready for use –
need not finish until the end of Activity 15, 'Pour tea through
strainer into cup', and could therefore take place parallel to
Activity 13, 'Leave to brew or infuse'. This would then enable us to
reduce the duration of Activity 8 by a further 1 minute and reduce

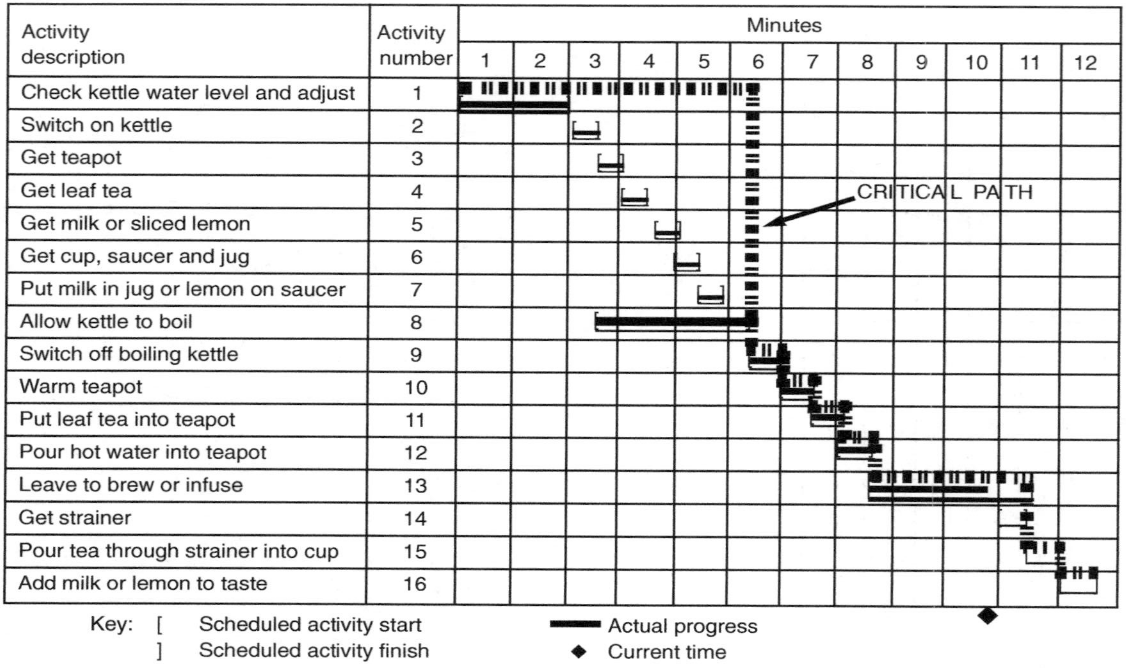

Figure 4.5 The English Project Gantt chart.

the overall project duration by a total of 2 minutes – from 11 minutes to 9 minutes.

The Gantt chart gives us a picture of the project that is clear and easily understood. Because of this it has remained one of the most popular forms of project plan, despite the more recent introduction of sophisticated and computerized network project planning systems. This popularity also reflects the fact that Gantt charts are easy to generate by hand – on standard graph paper or paper with pre-printed columns – and require limited training for their use. These characteristics make it particularly useful on small projects – in the home or the workplace. Proprietary versions of the wall mounted Gantt chart are available, having magnetic or special 'click in' strips, and are capable of displaying as many as one hundred activities. But the Gantt chart does have its limitations, the major one being that it cannot easily or clearly show activity interdependencies. As we saw earlier, interdependency occurs when one activity cannot start until another preceding activity has finished. Knowing which activities are interdependent is important, if not essential, to the effectiveness of our plan and the efficiency of its resource usage. Indeed, when you think about it you'll realize that most critical paths are sequences of interdependent activities. The updating or revision of a large manually generated Gantt chart takes time and this can also cause problems, particularly at a time when that updated or revised plan is urgently needed. However, computer generated Gantt charts can help in that sort of situation.

Despite these limitations the Gantt chart does have significant advantages and is often used on small projects because of its low training demands and ease of generation, and on both large and small projects because of its direct and easily understood visual image.

Networks

Network planning systems first became popular towards the end of the 1950s. The original systems were PERT (Programme

Evaluation and Review Technique), which was aimed at working out whether a project would finish by a certain time, and CPM (Critical Path Method) or CPA (Critical Path Analysis), which was concerned with the trade-offs between the project's time and cost. Since that time their use has become very widespread and, not surprisingly, a number of other network systems have evolved, such as the Precedence Diagramming Method (PDM) or Activity on Node (AON) network, GERT (Graphical Evaluation and Review Technique) and VERT (Venture Evaluation and Review Technique). All of these have their particular uses and advantages (see 'Taking It Further' for relevant texts and web sites).

Activity on Arrow (AOA) networks

The Activity on Arrow (AOA) network or Arrow Diagramming Method (ADM) is an easily understood system of network planning that, for small projects, can be generated by hand or on a desk-top computer. AOA plans use a structured network to describe both the sequence of the project activities and the connections between those activities. Each of the activities is represented by an arrow and these are arranged so that they flow from left to right. Both the start and finish of an activity – or arrow – are marked by a circle – or node. These nodes are used, as we will see later, to store information about the duration of both the project and the activity.

Figure 4.6 shows a simple AOA network in which the activities are numbered 1, 2, 3, 4, 5 and 6 and the nodes – which are also called events – are identified by the letters a, b, c, d, e and f.

The rules for building these networks are simple and straightforward:

▶ *the finish of one activity is also the start of the following activity – except at the end of the network*
▶ *activities can take place at the same time*
▶ *several activities can start from one event or merge into one event.*

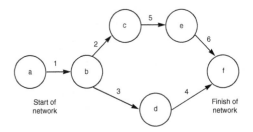

Figure 4.6 Simple AOA network.

But, as it stands, this example network doesn't tell us about how long these activities take, whether any of them are interdependent or what the Critical Path is. To get to that point we need to know how long the activities take and what their dependencies are, as in Figure 4.7a. When we include this data in our network, it changes, as in Figure 4.7b. The dotted line (called a dummy activity) tells us that Activity 6 cannot start until both Activities 3 and 5 are complete.

But this still doesn't give us all the information that we need. In order to get that we have to do some calculations. The results of these will tell us what is the earliest time that an event can take place, the 'earliest event time' or EET, and what is the latest time

Activity	Duration [hr]	Can only be completed after Activity
1	2	–
2	2.75	1
3	3.5	1
4	4	3
5	1	2
6	2	3 & 5

Figure 4.7a Activity dependencies and durations.

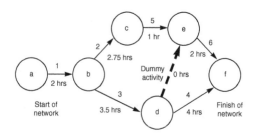

Figure 4.7b Simple AOA network with activity durations and dummy activity.

that an event can take place, the 'latest event time' or LET. To store this and other information in the network we have to change the circles – or nodes – to look like Figure 4.8.

The data for the EET and the LET of each node are generated as follows:

▶ *Start at the first event of the network and write the figure 'o' in the EET location.*
▶ *Moving to event b, add the duration of activity 1 – which is 2 hrs – to the EET for event a – which is 0 – giving a total of 2 hrs and write this in the EET location for event b.*
▶ *Follow through the network adding each activity duration to the previous EET and writing the resultant figure into the EET location of the relevant finish activity node.*
▶ *When you reach an event where two activities merge, as at e or f, write in the highest figure generated for the EET. Note that dummy activities have a zero duration.*
▶ *Continue to the last event and write the figure generated in both the EET and the LET locations of the last node.*
▶ *Starting from event f, trace the network backwards, subtracting the duration of the following activity from the LET at each event and writing the figure generated in the LET location in the node at the event's start.*
▶ *When you reach an event at which two activities merge, as at d or b, write in the lowest LET calculated.*

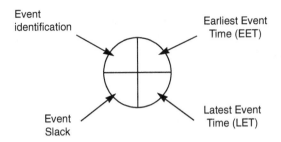

Figure 4.8 AOA network node.

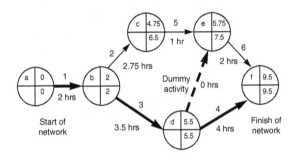

Figure 4.9 Calculating EET and LET.

▶ Continue this through to the first event – at which you should have a LET which is the same as the EET for this event. If you haven't, then you've made a mistake – probably at an event where two or more activities merge.

The figures we calculate will give us a network that looks like the one in Figure 4.9. Check your network against it.

You'll notice that some of the arrows in this network are heavy and bold. These represent the sequence of activities that defines the overall project duration, i.e. the project critical path. You'll also be able to see – because event f has an EET and an LET that are both equal to 9.5 – that the project will take 9.5 hours to complete. But, if we look carefully, we will also see that activity 2 – which starts after 2 hours of project time – could finish at 2 + 2.75 = 4.75 hours but doesn't need to finish until 6.5 hours. Similarly activity 5 could finish at 4.75 + 1 = 5.75 hours but need not finish until 7.5 hours. These differences – between the time required and the time available for an activity – are called the 'float' or 'slack' of that activity.

This 'float' or 'slack' is useful to the ways that we schedule the project activities. For example, we could delay the start of activity 5 until the LET (6.5 hours) of its start node or start at the original time – 4.75 hours – and extend the duration of the activity by using fewer people or a different method, up to a maximum of 7.5 – 4.75 = 2.75 hours. In the full AOA network float is shown in the network nodes and the resulting network looks like Figure 4.10.

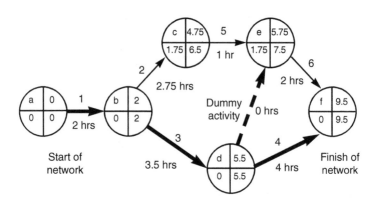

Figure 4.10 Full AOA network.

So far we have assumed that we know, with certainty, how long our activities will take. But this isn't always so. We might, for example, be working with estimated durations whose values range from 'best' to 'worst' or from 'shortest' to 'longest'. When this happens we can calculate what is called an 'expected duration' for each activity and then use those to generate the network. To do this we use the following equation:

$$\text{Expected activity duration} = \frac{(a + 4m + b)}{6}$$

where:

- ▶ *a = estimated shortest activity duration*
- ▶ *b = estimated longest activity duration*
- ▶ *m = most likely activity duration.*

Despite the fact that it has a lower level of visual impact than the Gantt chart, the Activity on Arrow network enables us to work out the results of network changes, as when, for example, an activity duration increases, without redrawing the network. This means that we can quickly examine the trade-offs between outcome, time, cost and quality. However, training and experience are needed if we are to make efficient and effective use of the AOA network. Despite this, the AOA network, in its computer-driven form, is often used on large and complex projects and, in the manually or computer generated form, used for the small projects of our homes and workplaces.

Activity on Node (AON) networks

The basic elements of an AON network look like this:

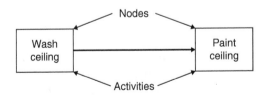

Figure 4.11 Activity on Node example.

When this is used to generate a full AON network, what you get is the sort of network that's shown in Figure 4.12.

The information carried in each of these nodes is generated in the same way as that for the AOA network except that the backward pass generates latest start times rather than latest event times. The AON network has no equivalent to the dummy activity of the AOA network and activity D is shown as being dependent upon activities C and B.

The advantages of the AON network include:

▶ *its ability to cope with change – since information rather then the network has to be changed*
▶ *its ability to provide the project manager with trade-off related information*
▶ *the speed – relative to AOA networks – of its computer driven versions.*

Its disadvantages include:

▶ *complex calculations involved*
▶ *network diagrams are not easy to understand or follow*
▶ *considerable training and experience needed for effective use.*

Because of these factors, AON networks tend to be used in a computer driven form and on large and complex projects.

Resources

So far, we have looked at two of the ways in which we can plan the project's use of time. But if we think about it we will soon realize that the Gantt chart and the AOA network both assume that the resources required for the project's activities are always available in the required quantity at the right time.

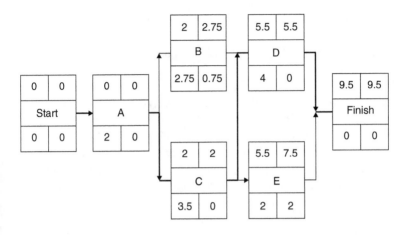

KEY:

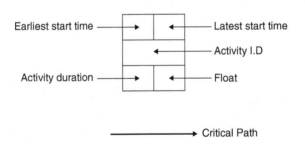

Earliest start time ——————— Latest start time
————— Activity I.D
Activity duration ——————— Float

————————→ Critical Path

Figure 4.12 Simple AON network.

In reality, resource availability doesn't always reach that pinnacle
of performance. The crane that we need might be in use elsewhere
or the grade of paper we want might not be in stock. Some of
these resourcing dilemmas might have their roots in the ways in
which we plan. For example, as we saw in Chapter 1, the resource
demands of the project can vary throughout its life cycle – with
those of the Production phase often exceeding those of the other
phases by several orders of magnitude. This might mean that we
run out of booked mainframe computer time during this stage
because we based our estimates on an average rate of usage. We
may also have resourcing problems because we haven't taken into
account the limitations that are built into the resources themselves
or the task – such as the well known impossibility of getting
ten men to dig, in one day, a hole which it would take one man
ten days to complete.

In general, though, our resourcing difficulties come about
either because we are short of time and need more resources
to compensate, or because we don't have enough resources
available, as when the promised delivery fails to materialize.
What we need to do now is to look at how we can overcome
these situations.

Activity slack

We saw earlier that we are able to regulate the way in which
we complete an activity with slack or float either by delaying
the start of the activity and using original resource level or by
using the original start time and extending the activity duration by
using fewer or different resources. This is called 'resource levelling'.

Slack is the term used in PERT for float.

We can use it to smooth the project's pattern of resource usage. This means that there will be fewer (and smaller) peaks and troughs in that pattern. As we saw in our earlier English Project, this process of resource levelling for small projects is simple enough. The calculations involved can be done on a desk or pocket calculator – or even in your head! However, as the number of activities involved in the project increases, this process becomes more and more complicated. As a result, computers and specialized software are usually used for large or complex projects.

What did we do last time?

Sometimes we are faced with the need to decide which of many project activities we will use our scarce resource on. When this happens there often isn't enough time to undertake a reasoned and logical analysis. This is particularly true of the scarce resource allocation problems which are common in development projects, in which resource demand patterns are volatile and changeful. It would just take too long to look at all the options and choose the best solution. Under these circumstances we use heuristics or 'rules of thumb' to solve our problems.

These are rules that have, in the past, produced good results. They are also easy to understand and apply. Examples of the rules for our projects range from the obvious – 'Do critical path activities first' or 'Do activities with most subsequent critical path activities first' – to the less obvious – 'Do activities with smallest float first' and 'Do shortest activities first'. All of these represent simple and realistic solutions that can be applied quickly and cheaply to the resource problems that our projects generate.

Project planning with computers

There was a time – believe it or not! – when projects were planned without the help of computers.

Now, of course, things are different – we all own or have access to high-powered desktop computers. There can be little doubt that these have completely changed the ways in which we plan our projects. But computer technology never stays still and we are always being offered new, better and faster computers and upgraded, modernized software packages to run on them. Because of this, any attempt to survey all of these and guide you towards what might be a 'best buy' for project planning would not only be foolish, it would be out of date before this book was published!

Instead, this book will identify some of the factors you need to be clear about before you choose your project planning software package. This is an important step and it is often overlooked or given scant attention in the helter-skelter rush to buy the newest software.

Firstly, you need to think about your projects – about their size and complexity. Try, for example, to decide if they involve more than 500 activities or use multiple resources or if there is a high level of uncertainty about activity durations. Ask yourself if you'll need to keep people outside the project team informed about project progress and, if so, at what level of detail. Try to decide if you'll need to update the project plan frequently or to use resource smoothing or allocation. When you've got the answers to these questions then you're ready to move on to thinking about the sort of software that you need.

Insight
Computers and software packages do not give you planning skills – these come when you use these tools well.

There are all sorts of project planning software packages on the market. Most, but not all of them, are designed to do just what you'd expect them to do – help you to plan your project. But the ways in which they do it are different and it's these differences that will lead you to buy one package or to reject another. The ease with which you can enter, model and schedule your project will be, for some of you, the critical factor in your choice. For others, it will be whether the package can handle costs or resources or a particular sort of report.

What you have to do is to identify the characteristics of the package that you want. Do you, for example, want it to be capable of generating AOA networks and Gantt charts or AON and Precedence diagram networks? Try to work out how many activities and nodes you want it to be able to handle and decide what sort of limitations you will accept in the way that these are identified. The range of calendar time that's built into the software is important as is its ability to smooth or allocate resources and handle costs and sub-projects.

High levels of user friendliness are vital – but you don't want to get lost in a maze of menus. The software's outputs and reports must tell you and your clients what you both want to know. You'll need an understandable but comprehensive manual and software support – as and when you need it.

Finally, do make sure that the software you choose is compatible with your computer – its speed, hard disk capacity, RAM size and operating system version can be important. It's worth looking at several programmes and trialling these so that you get a good feel for what they can and can't do. In the Project Planning Computer Software Checklist below there's a list of aspects opposite you'll want to bear in mind when you do this. While your 'shopping list' of these software packages will probably include such popular, versatile and well proven packages as Artemis, MS Project, Merlin, Cresta and Open Plan it's important that you find one that:

▶ *you are comfortable with*
▶ *produces the sort of results that you want.*

It's just as important that you put some time and effort into getting to know your chosen program's idiosyncrasies and quirks – before you use it for real.

Project planning computer software checklist

Use this list in your assessment of project planning software.

Network/chart:
- ▶ Gantt chart
- ▶ AOA
- ▶ AON
- ▶ All or most of above

Calendar:
- ▶ Range of years
- ▶ Number of working days/weeks
- ▶ Non-working days (statutory holidays, etc.)

Events/activities:
- ▶ Maximum number
- ▶ Identification restraints (alpha-numeric, number of characters)

Access, ease of use and support:
- ▶ Menus
- ▶ Help screens/website
- ▶ Data entry
- ▶ User manual
- ▶ User hot line
- ▶ Training
- ▶ User group/blog

Reports:
- ▶ Standard report range
- ▶ User defined reports
- ▶ Graphics

Resources:	▶ Resource allocation
	▶ Resource range
	▶ Resource type
Operating	▶ Current
System:	▶ Known updates due
	▶ Future proof
	▶ Firewall/virus proofing
Hardware:	▶ Needs new?
	▶ Current OK?

What next?

Now you can move on to look at some of the things that you need to know about and do in order to manage your project. But, before you do that, read through the following list – this chapter's ten most important messages.

TOP TEN MESSAGES

1 *Your project plan enables you to convert the objectives of your project into concrete realities and outcomes.*

2 *To create that plan you need to know the:*
   ▷ *what*
   ▷ *when*
   ▷ *who*
   ▷ *with what*
   of the project's actions.

3 *You also need to know about your project's:*
   ▷ *budgeted cost*
   ▷ *level of outcome quality.*

4 *A Gantt chart gives you a picture of the project that is clear and easily understood.*

5 *An Activity on Arrow (AOA) network is an easily understood system of planning.*

6 *An Activity on Node (AON) network is well able to cope with change.*

7 *Small projects often use Gantt charts or AOA networks.*

8 *Large or complex projects usually use AOA or AON networks.*

9 *The resource usage of your project can be planned and managed by using:*
   ▷ *resource smoothing*
   ▷ *heuristic rules.*

10 *Make sure that the project planning software package that you choose answers your needs.*

5

Managing your project

In this chapter you will learn:
- *About the role of the project manager*
- *The difference between the role of project manager and day-to-day manager*
- *What skills the project manager needs*

Management

Management is about organizing people and things so that they generate the results that we want.

The role of the manager is a very common one. We have presidents, prime ministers, archbishops, superintendents, football coaches, work group co-ordinators, office managers, baseball team managers, restaurant managers and rail station supervisors – and these are all managers. But what, if anything, do they have in common?

Insight
Good managers work hard at making sure people know what they are trying to achieve.

To find an answer to that question we first have to recognize that the manager is a creature of our organizations. These, as we saw in Chapter 3, have structures, roles and responsibilities. The manager is one of the most important of these roles. He or she has a formal authority over the whole or part of the organization. This gives him or her power, status and access to information and resources. But these are not unconditional gifts. For the organization expects that the manager will only use these to achieve its objectives – whatever these might be. The people who act as managers are selected and appointed – a process that assesses an individual's abilities and skills and compares them to those thought to be needed to do the job. The formality and visibility of this process can vary: in some organizations it is a 'behind closed doors' process, while in others it is a very public and open process in which all stakeholders are involved.

There are many views about what a manager does. However, the majority of them seem to agree that the manager:

- ▶ *displays leadership and authority*
- ▶ *monitors and disseminates information*
- ▶ *takes decisions and resolves conflicts.*

Managing projects versus day-to-day management

We have already seen the Five Fundamentals of the project – its one-off nature, its limited and defined time span, its uniqueness, its defined outcome and its focus on change. The organization is different. As we saw in Chapter 3, its prime concern lies in survival and in ensuring that it can continue to produce – repeatedly and accurately – replicas or hybrids of its products or services. These differences begin to give us clues about the different ways in which the project and the organization need to be managed.

For organizations are primarily concerned with stability, continuity and repetition. Their day-to-day operations take in customers or materials and process or service them in ways that are routine and often fixed. The resources – equipment, buildings – that are used in these operations are also fixed and static to ensure their consistent availability. The managers of these operations are concerned with continuity and consistency and satisfying the often conflicting needs of the task, the organization, the customer and his or her staff. Doing this involves trade-offs between the factors of cost, time, output and even quality.

In contrast, the management of our projects is concerned with creating and sustaining change. Resources come and go, as required. The project manager has little freedom to exercise trade-offs – because her or his project has a fixed, finite, limited time scale, cost and outcome. As a consequence, her or his skill and judgement are exercised in ways that are far more focused. On the average project there are few opportunities to reverse out of your mistakes.

Most, but not all, day-to-day managers are or have been functional specialists. They are or were engineers, production specialists, accountants, nurses, sales managers, marketers, designers, bankers or personal finance specialists. Now they manage departments, sections and groups dedicated to those functions. The project manager, however, is a generalist, a facilitator, an enabler. The project manager rarely has in-depth specialist knowledge; she or he oversees specialists and facilitates the contributions that their expertise makes to the project.

All of these differences between the project manager and the day-to-day manager lead us to the point at which we can see that project management is about the management of exceptions rather than, as in day-to-day management, management by exception, in which a manager only intervenes in operations under his or her control when exceptional or problematic situations arise. We might almost say that the effective project manager surfs on, exploits and uses the waves of change while the day-to-day manager strives to steer a steady course whatever the 'weather'. Of course, both have their places in our world but the ways in which they operate are very different. Because of these differences, projects must be organized, planned and managed in ways that differ from those that we use in our day-to-day activities – as we will see in the chapters that follow.

Projects and managers

Managers and projects come together either because the manager takes over and manages the completed project's outcome or because she or he is responsible for the management of the project itself.

It's the second of those roles – that of the project manager – that we will look at now.

Insight

A project manager is rather like a band leader in that she or he makes sure that everyone associated with the project is playing from the same sheet and to the same beat.

The project is the most effective way of creating change. Managing it well demands a diverse and unique set of skills and experience. The project manager needs to be a broad view generalist, able to integrate or bring things together – creating, for example, a whole project from its disparate parts. To be effective the project manager must be:

▶ *familiar with and able to use project management tools and techniques*
▶ *able to make sure that the project's money is spent in ways that maximize its benefit to the project*
▶ *skilled in fostering co-operative working relationships within the project team and with all the project stakeholders*
▶ *able to identify risks and act in ways to limit their effects upon the project.*

This is a demanding and stressful role. It is said that the only comfortable and relaxed project manager is either one who is waiting for her or his next project or one who is on the edge of failure in their current one. It is, nevertheless, a role which exerts significant influence upon both the direction of and the potential for success of the project.

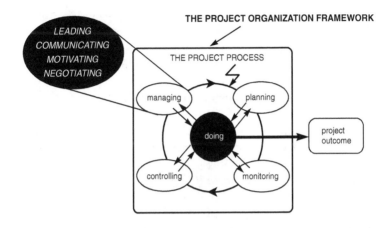

Figure 5.1 Managing and the project process.

In order to do this the project manager must be able to:

▶ *lead – a team of skilled individuals*
▶ *communicate – with everyone who is involved in the project*
▶ *motivate – the project team, contractors and sub-contractors*
▶ *negotiate – effective solutions to the conflicts that arise between the needs of the project and its stakeholders.*

These skills are needed whether our project is large or small, to do with our workplace or our home, and worth a small fortune or a pittance.

Leaders and leadership

Somebody once said that leadership is about persuading people to do what they should have done in the first place. It's also about the ways in which we influence the thoughts and actions of others.

This can come about because of our role in an organization, as sales supervisor, production manager or CEO, or because of our personality, as in the 'charisma' that we possess. In each of these situations we exert influence on others, either because of the authority given to our role or because we behave in ways or say things that attract them or that they wish to emulate.

But these aren't the only ways by which we can influence people. We can also influence what people do or say because:

- ▶ *we are able to punish them if they act in ways other than those that we approve of or desire*
- ▶ *we are an expert in a certain field*
- ▶ *we are able to grant (or withhold) benefits or things they desire*
- ▶ *we have access to others who might also do all or any of the above.*

By now you've probably spotted that other people than leaders can do some of these. A manager, for example, can dismiss you or give you a raise and a supervisor can be an expert in welding or word processing.

> **Insight**
> 'Management is doing things right; leadership is doing the right things.' (Peter Drucker)

But being a manager or a supervisor isn't the same thing as being a leader. A manager is about forecasting, planning, organizing, commanding, co-ordinating and controlling, whereas being a leader is about something else. The leaders are people who exert a directing influence or guidance; they can exert this influence about matters that are spiritual, political, national or commercial. They inspire us by creating visions of desired futures. Being able to do this is a rare skill and because of this there are far more managers than leaders. Indeed, a true leader – one who creates such a response in us that we, literally, would follow him or her – is a very rare bird.

But when we think about this we will soon realize that being a manager and being a leader aren't mutually exclusive – we can manage and we can also lead. But being one doesn't automatically mean that you are or can be the other. Being good at leading doesn't necessarily mean that you are good at managing, or vice versa. Perhaps the right way, for most of us, is a combination of the two – the ability to influence backed up by the ability to plan, organize, co-ordinate and control.

So, then, given that most of us know how to manage, how can we become more of a leader?

There was a time when the answer to this question would have been that you can't become a leader – either you are one or you aren't. This view – that leaders are born and not made – was popular for a long time. But years of dedicated research by many people failed to come up with an adequate answer to what it is in your background or genetics that makes you a leader. Bearing this in mind and remembering our starting point – that leading others is about influencing them – we begin to see that leadership is not as simple and straightforward as some would have us believe. The textbooks of management contain many, many views of the ways that leading is, or ought to be, carried out. While the good thing about all this is that it gets us away from the 'leaders are born' school of thought, the bad thing is that the many styles of leadership identified can be confusing. However, there does seem to be a consensus that the style of leadership that is appropriate depends upon a number of things. Amongst the more significant of these we find:

▶ *the location in which the leadership is being applied*
▶ *the culture of the organization*
▶ *what the task is or what's being done*
▶ *how the followers like to be led.*

All of this means that there isn't a single unique style of leadership that will always produce the best results. As they say, it all depends.

When we think about this it begins to make sense. We know (or can imagine) that the style of leadership that is appropriate to a battlefield situation is different from that used in the 'work-a-day' office situation. The leadership style that works when a team is doing a routine task is different from the one needed when the team task demands high levels of creativity. Effective leadership takes into account and answers the needs of both the task in hand and the group working on that task.

Because our projects are one-off unique events, this means that there is no single 'right' style of project leadership. Instead, there is a range of different styles, some of which will work with certain projects and project teams but will not work with other projects or project teams.

Insight
Try to be the sort of leader that people look for – rather than steer clear of.

An effective project team leader takes into account the nature of the project, the prior experience and composition of the project team and the project's time, money, and quality constraints. Large projects mean big teams. These need to be organized in ways that are different from the ways that we organize the teams of small projects. Experienced project teams will need less direction than inexperienced ones and teams who have worked together before may (or may not!) work together better than teams of strangers. The projects of our homes will demand leadership that is different from the leadership used in the projects of our workplaces.

In the end, effective project leadership is about getting the required results as and when they are needed. If the project manager is going to achieve that then she or he must be able and willing to communicate with the people involved in that project – and this we will now look at.

Project managers and communication

The boardroom and the bedroom are two of the places that shout for effective communication. But they're not the only ones.

Communication is key to all of our lives. We need to 'get our message across' to everyone – work colleagues, partners, customers, children, parents, teachers and doctors. But in some of the roles that we carry out, effective communication is the primary skill.

One of these is the role of the project manager. Project managers spend a lot of their time communicating. They do it with almost everyone involved in the project. The list is almost endless – client managers, contractors, project team members, union officials, government inspectors. All of these and others have to be listened to, explained to, informed, sold ideas and persuaded.

Insight

Communication is the glue that holds your project together.

Communication has, at its core, the act of exchanging information. A rich and complex two-way process with an interplay of message and reply, of input and feedback, it uses both the written word, as in letters, memos and reports, and the spoken word, as when we speak to each other face to face or over the telephone. We also inform each other through our gestures, movements, expressions, postures and gaze.

Project communications

The communications that take place in our projects are important. They enable us to exchange facts, broker information, exert influence and even, on occasions, to express emotions. They are both formal and informal in nature.

The formal communications of the project are targeted at answering the information needs of the project stakeholders. As such they should be planned with care and precision. That planning should identify who needs what, when it's needed and what form it's needed in. Issues such as the immediacy of information needs – as in e-mail or snail mail – and the technology involved – as in

Internet or Intranet – should be debated and resolved. These formal communications should be about the project performance. As such, they should give the project stakeholders information about:

- *what work has been done since the last communication*
- *what work should have been done in that period*
- *what work is planned for the next period.*

They should also provide up-to-date information on the cost performance of the project such as the budgeted and actual spend to date, the budgeted spend to completion, etc. This information can be expressed as bar charts (see Chapter 4), S curves, schedule and cost variance reports or Earned Value reports (see Chapter 8). The formal communications of the project can take place in meetings or be generated in hard copy or electronic form. Meetings are held to review project progress and can be actual or video conferenced. Which you choose will depend upon the size of the project and the availability of networked information systems.

The informal communications of the project are just as important as the formal ones. But they are often underrated or taken for granted. They take place in the innumerable casual conversations, telephone calls, chats and discussions that litter our days. They are accidental, unplanned, fortuitous and spontaneous. They are, however, the ways and means of most of our communications. The ways in which they are used by the project manager can be crucial to the success of the project. The project manager is not wasting her or his time when she or he visits, in the early days of the project, everybody who has anything to do with the project. She or he is laying down the framework of an informal communications network that will, in future days, be crucial to the success of the project.

Skill in the 'art' of communication is a must for all project managers. They all, if they are to be effective, must be able to write, speak, listen to and read body, spoken and written language with skill and ability. Effective communication can make a considerable contribution to the success of the project.

Project managers and negotiation

We are all negotiators. We learn to do it 'at our mother's knee'. We continue to use and develop our negotiating skills throughout the rest of our lives. The things that we negotiate about reflect every aspect of our lives and these negotiations take place everyday and everywhere we work and play.

The project manager is no exception to this. His or her negotiations are about every aspect of the project. They can be structured and formal – resulting in written agreements – or informal and about generating verbal understandings. All of these negotiations take place because of the conflict that occurs when the drives that we all have, to achieve goals that answer our needs, are frustrated. When this happens, strife and argument arise. Then, we need to find a way forward. For if we fail to resolve these conflicts they will divert the energy and drive of the project team away from what should be its primary objective – achieving the project's goals. The key lies in the art of negotiation.

Negotiating and bargaining

When we negotiate with someone we become involved in a search. It's a search to find, firstly, general areas of agreement and acceptability and then, secondly, to identify specific outcomes that are acceptable.

But this is not a search that we conduct on our own. For the outcomes that we generate must, if they are to work, also be acceptable to those people that we are negotiating with. For not only are they the solutions to today's problems – they also define the ways in which we will interact in the future. Bargaining is an important part of this process. It involves us in haggling, dealing or bartering – acts with which we are all familiar.

The negotiations of our project can be about anything to do with that project. In its early stages they can be about such issues as the project's objectives or its organization. In later stages, plans, schedules and procedures, contracts, prices and priorities can be involved. By the end of the project they can be concerned with the detail of the project handover and the subsequent list of items needing corrective action.

The manner in which these negotiations are conducted and the quality of their outcomes are important. Negotiations with win–win endings have an influence beyond the bargaining table. They create a genuine shared will to succeed. This sort of negotiation starts by identifying areas of potential agreement.

Ways and means

In its simplest form, negotiating involves two people. It is a face-to-face debate on some matter of shared interest. Its outcome is a mutually acceptable settlement or compromise.

Let's, for the moment, imagine that two people – A and B – are negotiating about the sale of some land. A would like to sell the land and B wants to buy it. Their shared objective is to try to find out if they can agree on a price. But as we watch them we begin to realize that there isn't just one price involved. B, for example, will have one price which she or he is not prepared to exceed and another, lower, price that she or he hopes to buy at. A will also have two prices: the one below which she or he is not prepared to sell and another, higher one, which she or he hopes to sell for. But neither knows what the other's prices are and they open the process of negotiation with the first of a series of offers and counter offers. B will offer to buy at a very low cost and A will reject that, countering with a very high offer to sell. The levels of these offers are chosen so that they can be changed and, in so doing, appear to be offering compromise. This process of offer–counter offer will continue with B attempting to pull down A's price, if possible to his or her 'hoped for' cost, while A will attempt to push B's offers up, again, if possible, to the level of his or her 'hoped for' price. When we watch the tactics and games that are used during this offer–counter offer sequence we might see A giving ground slowly and reluctantly in response to B's threats of withdrawal. These threats might be countered by A invoking things like other offers, company policy or saying that there is nothing left to give. The final position that is reached in this game of push and pull will depend upon how skilled and experienced the negotiators are, whether there are alternative sellers or buyers and what prices had been agreed in other, similar, negotiations. If it's a win–lose negotiation, rather than a win–win one, then you can also add the incentive created by whoever lost last time not wishing to repeat the experience.

In most negotiations A and B would, by now, have entered what is often called the **bargaining zone** (see Figure 5.2). The upper boundary of this zone is the maximum price that B (the buyer) is prepared to pay and its lower boundary is the minimum price that A (the seller) is prepared to accept. Obviously, if B's maximum is less than A's minimum, then the zone will not exist and the negotiation will fail. For A and B to enter this zone and achieve a successful win–win conclusion to their negotiation requires real skill and commitment on both their parts. They will need to be able to create a relationship which is built on mutual trust. In order to do that they must be able to identify not only what is happening but also why it is happening and what needs to be done about it. They will also need to be able to communicate with each other with clarity and precision and listen without bias or prejudice.

The project manager is involved in negotiations at every stage of the project's life cycle and the way in which she or he negotiates can make a considerable difference to the success of the project.

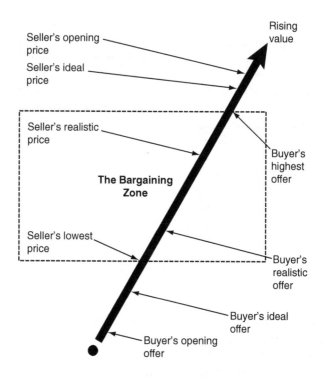

Figure 5.2 The bargaining zone.

Project managers and motivation

Motivation is what gives our behaviour direction and purpose.

When we are motivated to do something – or 'turned on' to it – it is usually because we think that doing it will lead to us getting something that we want. Motivation is a complex process and the question of what motivates people to perform effectively is not an easy one to answer.

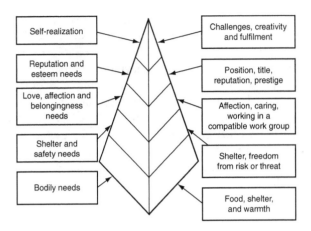

Figure 5.3 Maslow's Hierarchy of Needs.

One of the more accessible views about this was that of Abraham Maslow. His view was that human beings are in a state of incessant need. For almost all of us, these needs are only partially satisfied. It is this state of unsatisfaction that drives us to act in the ways that we do. Maslow suggested that these needs, which he classified into five basic groups, are arranged or 'stacked', one above another, as in a pyramid (Figure 5.3).

On the base of this pyramid are our physical needs – for food, warmth and shelter. These are followed by our needs for shelter, protection and security and then our affection and attachment needs. Towards the top of the pyramid are our needs for reputation and recognition. Finally, at the top, is our need for self-realization. These need groups are said to act upon us in their order in the pyramid and are at their most potent when they are unsatisfied. For example, we have to satisfy our basic need for warmth, food, water and shelter before we begin to seek 'higher' needs such as job security, prestige and the freedom to create. However, this is not a totally rigid structure and there are, as Maslow pointed out, people for whom self-esteem is more important than love or for whom the fulfilment of their creative needs overrides all other needs.

So, can we apply this view of motivation to our projects? The answer is yes, but a conditional yes. However, we do need to be aware that people are not as simple or as straightforward as this theory appears to suggest. The enormous complexity shown by people every day challenges the apparent simplicity of this 'pyramid' of needs. But, it does, nevertheless, provide us with some useful information. It tells us, for example, that people come to work for other needs than the money with which to answer their basic needs of food, warmth, shelter and security. They need, for example, to answer their social and their creative needs as well.

Insight

Motivation is about answering people's needs – or rather giving them the chance to answer their own needs.

The project manager who ignores these other 'higher' needs does so at his or her peril. A not-so-old saying confirms this when it tells us to 'find the right people and then get the hell out of their way'. A wise project manager recognizes and allows for the fact that people need to plan and control their own work and need to be involved in management decisions about that work.

Key people on the project manager's list of people to be motivated are the members of the project team. Teams are unusual and we will explore them in more detail in the next chapter. For the time being we need to note that team members can be motivated to perform better by either enlarging or enriching their jobs.

Role enlargement involves extending a role's duties or responsibilities. It happens, for example, when we ask the project electrical engineer to take on the responsibility for the project computers. Role enrichment, however, involves allocating more interesting or challenging duties to a role. It happens when we ask that electrical engineer to be responsible for decisions about major project contracts that are concerned with other than electrical engineering.

Motivating the project team, however it is achieved, is a key task for all project managers. It remains a simple but powerful truth that well-motivated project staff perform well and in so doing contribute to the success of the project. Use the checklist below to find your answer to the question, 'How good a project manager are you?'

How good a project manager are you?

Under each of the headings below ring the number which is nearest to the way that you feel that you manage your projects. Then add up your total and go to the Key section below.

1 Leadership

| I always lead my team the same way. | 1 2 3 4 5 6 7 | I try to work out which way is best for this team and this project. |

2 Communication

| I tell people what I think. | 1 2 3 4 5 6 7 | I listen when people talk and they listen when I talk. |

3 Organizing

| These things usually sort themselves out. | 1 2 3 4 5 6 7 | People have to know what to do, when and how to do it. |

4 Motivation

| We pay them, isn't that enough? | 1 2 3 4 5 6 7 | I see my team as creative problem solvers. |

5 Decision Taking

| I let problems solve themselves. | 1 2 3 4 5 6 7 | I decide quickly and with the information that I've got. |

(Contd)

What next?

Now you're going to move on – in the next chapter – to look at teams. You'll find out about the ways in which they do (and don't) work and the what and how of their contribution to your project. But, before you do that, read through the following list – this chapter's ten most important messages.

TOP TEN MESSAGES

1 *Management is about organizing people and things so that they produce the results that you want.*

2 *This act of managing things and people happens quite a lot in organizations.*

3 *When you are a manager, you'll display leadership and authority and monitor and disseminate information.*

4 *You'll also take decisions, resolve conflicts and negotiate.*

5 *To become a manager you need to be selected, appointed and given formal authority.*

6 *Carrying out the role of manager will give you status and mean that you are able to access information and resources.*

7 *The role of project manager is different from the day-to-day operations manager.*

8 *The project manager*
   ▷ *uses resources that are transient*
   ▷ *works to a time scale that is frozen*
   ▷ *creates a unique outcome*
   ▷ *is primarily concerned with the creation of change*
   ▷ *needs to be a gifted, broad-view generalist who can integrate or bring things together.*

9 *The project manager also needs to be able to:*
   ▷ *lead a team of skilled individuals*
   ▷ *communicate*
   ▷ *motivate the project team, contractors and sub-contractors*
   ▷ *negotiate effective solutions to the conflicts that arise in the project.*

10 *The effective project manager is key to the success of a project.*

6

Your project team

In this chapter you will learn:
- *About ways in which teams do (and don't) work*
- *About factors that influence team performance*
- *How successful teams can contribute to a project*

Why teams?

The team – or rather the team that works – gives us a way of working together that is both versatile and effective.

Insight

A great team is where 2+2 equals at least 5.

In all sorts of situations – at work, at play, and in the home – the team has a proven track-record of creativity and achievement. Most of us have experienced, at some point in our lives, that extra 'something' that a good team can create. A team that works well can, sometimes literally, 'move mountains'. This sort of a team takes our individual efforts and synergizes them into a greater whole. It is capable of growing, changing and adapting to meet new demands. It's also able to survive and even reinvent itself as, and when, individual members move on or its original task changes.

But experience also tells us that the team can be a difficult place to work in. For being a team member means that we have to give up some of our individuality – to submerge ourselves in a greater whole. It can also expose us to feedback about ourselves and our job performance – feedback that can be uncomfortable.

So why does the team exist and why do we use it? The answer is a simple one. Teams exist because they have the potential to outperform our individual efforts. Their performance also surpasses those of all the other sorts of social groups that exist in our organizations. Put simply, there is nothing to beat a good team – in terms of either performance or our experience of it!

It is this potential that is important to our projects. It can convert a moribund, mediocre project into a thriving, sparkling success. In this chapter we will look at what it is that gives a 'good' team that potential and how we can use it in the process of managing successful projects.

What is a team?

The word 'team' is, of course, a very common one. It's used on our sports fields, as in football, soccer, rugby, baseball and basketball teams, and in our workplaces, as in 'Finishing shop team' or 'Telephone sales team'. When we look it up in the dictionary we find the word 'team' is defined by phrases like 'a number of people' and verbs such as 'collaborating' and 'working together'. Teams generally have members with defined functional roles, such as 'goalkeeper', 'pitcher' or 'team leader', and what goes on inside them is often seen to be co-operative and constructive, as in 'team spirit' or 'team work'.

But isn't this the same as a group? The answer is no, it isn't. The word 'group' – which is defined as 'an assemblage of persons' who are 'standing together' – is used to describe a number of people with a purpose or interest in common. Examples are a group of baseball fans or a group of theatre-goers. The team – which also consists of people – is different. Its members have a purpose that is generated by consensus and debate. Because of that, the purpose is shared by the team. People in groups act as individuals, following their own individual desires and needs. Team members act together in ways that are co-operative and aimed at generating outcomes that are desired by the whole team rather than any one individual. The outcomes that teams generate are often definable, even measurable 'products' – such as a design for a new car or a completed project. Group outcomes are much more 'fuzzy' and generalized – such as 'influence' or 'power'.

These differences continue in our workplaces. Here, groups have a strong functional flavour, as in the Marketing or the Accounts Department, and their composition and size reflect the demands of that function. They also almost always have leaders – a role that remains with a single individual who is formally appointed. Their meetings are formal, structured, orderly events that delegate work to others outside the meeting.

Our workplace teams, however, are task focused. Their leadership is less formal – even to the point of being shared – with the leader role moving around the team as the availability of individuals or the phase of task in hand changes. Their meetings are usually open-ended, untidy debates aimed at solving problems.

All of this tells us that it's the team – rather than the group – that we want in our projects. For the team provides us with a way to tap into and harness the efforts, skills, abilities and creativity of all who are involved. This is true for all our projects – whether at work, at home or at play. The team has a considerable potential to contribute to their success.

However, teams don't always succeed and what we now need to begin to look at is what it takes to create and manage a 'good' team.

Good teams and bad teams

First, the bad news: the team, despite its considerable potential, doesn't always walk on water.

There are times and places when it doesn't work. This often happens when it's misapplied or used inappropriately, resulting in disruption and a waste of time and money. It can also be badly managed so that the initiative and creativity of individual team members are suppressed, inhibited or even overwhelmed. A team can lose touch with reality, creating its own set of values and ways of seeing the world, leading to outcomes that are not compatible with or desired by the real world outside.

But, despite all of this, the team is here to stay. This is because, at its best, the team is one of the most flexible and productive mechanisms for empowering and enabling people. It produces results that are not only desired by our organizations – they are essential to their survival. The team and performance go together like sugar and spice – different, but an unbeatable combination.

So, how do we create and manage a 'good' team? The answer to this question is, as usual, a mixture. In this case, the ingredients are common-sense and best practice. Our workplace teams exist within our organizations. As such they are influenced by the values, culture and 'ethos' of those organizations. These can act on the teams in different ways. They can encourage and support them – or they can limit their performance. For example, an organization that values performance, even above other values or standards, will be one in which teams will work well. It's the need for performance that counts – the team is the means rather than the end. But performance on its own is not enough – it has to be meaningful performance, performance that the team considers to be important.

Insight

'Only when all contribute their firewood can they have a strong fire.' (Chinese proverb)

That organization also has to be one in which individualism is prized but not at the expense of team membership. A 'good' team will not reject our individual creativity. It will find ways and means of accepting and using it. Nor will a good team operate in isolation. It will act and interact in ways that answer the needs of those around it.

In order to do that, the team has to be the 'right' size and have the 'right' mix of team members.

How many

Size is an important aspect of team operation. Get it wrong – as in too big or too small – and you'll limit the effectiveness of the team. Too big a team means that its members won't just have trouble in communicating effectively with each other, they'll also have difficulty in taking decisions and solving problems in ways that tap into, or make use of, the skills and knowledge of all the team members. Too small a team and you'll find yourself short on skills, expertise and people-time, despite the fact that you can communicate easily with each other.

So what is the 'right' number? The pragmatic answer is that it – the 'right' number for your team – lies within a range. What influences the size of your project team are factors such as the demands of the project task, the availability of the 'right' people and the sort of project organization that you've chosen.

Here are some guide lines.

Best practice seems to indicate that if you go above twenty-five members, then you're not talking about a team any more. But if you go below three members, then you'll run the risk of running short of relevant skills and experience and people-time. In general, the consensus seems to be that it's worthwhile limiting your team size to ten people.

But even that isn't a 'golden' number – to be applied whatever the team's task is. For example, for tasks in which member participation and involvement are key issues, such as joint union/ management study teams, the evidence is that the team size should be limited to between five and seven members. Other studies of

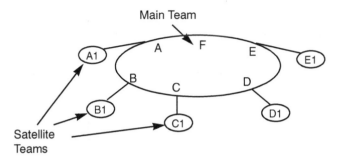

Figure 6.1 Main and satellite teams.

teams indicate that, if we want to harness the efforts, skills, abilities and creativity of our team members, then we have to limit the size of the team to between six and eight people. This may mean that, on large projects or projects with high staffing levels, we need to organize ourselves so that we have a series of interconnected teams with main team members chairing or leading the satellite teams and taking responsibility for the smooth and easy flow of information between the main and satellite teams, as illustrated in Figure 6.1.

Getting the size of the team right is not, however, the only factor. We also have to make sure that we have the right mix of people.

Who – and why

We all work in different ways. Some of us are analytical, logical, careful and considered in the ways that we work. We make our decisions with care and after due consideration of all the facts. Others make decisions quickly, almost impulsively, relying upon instinct or 'gut feelings'. But neither of these, nor the many other ways of taking decisions, are 'right'. More importantly, none of them is 'wrong'. They are simply different from each other.

But the differences between us aren't just about the ways in which we take decisions. We also behave in different ways, have different values, believe in different things, have different likes and dislikes and communicate in different ways. Some of these are compatible with each other and some are not.

All of this rich and abundant diversity means that the job of selecting the 'right people' for your team is important. Get it wrong and you'll have conflicts, difficulties and a poor team performance; get it right and you'll still have conflicts and difficulties but you'll also have a team that works.

Having said all of that, I'm also aware that some of you may not have the freedom to choose your own teams. You may have inherited them from a previous project manager or may have been given a team chosen by those above you in your organization. Your project team may consist of members of your family or a few willing volunteers. In these circumstances it's important that you take time out from the business of the project to find ways of working together. If you've inherited a team, there may be resentment about your 'taking over' from or even 'usurping' the previous team leader. It's important that you face that early and get the team to recognize that you need them – and they need you.

Insight

'Do you want a collection of brilliant minds or a brilliant collection of minds?' (R. Meredith Belbin)

Unfortunately the news that teams need to be selected carefully, and as a whole, hasn't reached everywhere. Many of our organizations select their teams using the criteria of functional skill only. This ignores the person behind that functional skill. In other situations people get chosen for teams because they are easy to get on with, do what they are told, don't rock the boat, etc. This, of course, ignores the issues of functional skill and creativity.

If we are to choose a successful team then we need to use some basic and relevant entry criteria. Of course, team members need to have the required functional skills. But they also need to have demonstrated their ability to work co-operatively with others when making decisions or solving problems and be willing to give up part of their own 'ego-space' in order to become integrated in the team. This task of integration into the team is not an easy one. One way of overcoming its difficulties is to pick people as team members because of all the above plus their ability to carry out at least one of the roles that a balanced team needs. These are generally about things like coming up with new ideas, defusing conflict or tension, looking after the team chores, analysing what's happening or even challenging the position of the rest of the team. If you think about it you'll soon realize that 'good' teams have all these roles and, as a result, can operate in ways that are independent of individual efforts or skills.

Finding out whether potential team members are up to these sorts of role, as well as meeting the basic entry criteria that we identified earlier, isn't an easy task. But, there is a surprising amount of information about. You can find out, for example, how they've performed in other teams, what their attitudes and responses have been to relevant training and development programmes or what their current or ex-bosses think about their team skills. You can also use one of the commercial team role assessment questionnaires – such as the Belbin Team Roles, MTR–i™ and Margerison-McCann questionnaires – that are available (see 'Taking it further' at end of the book).

The task of selecting a team is key to its success. With the right mixture of complementary skills, abilities and experience, the team has a potential that exceeds, by orders of magnitude, the sum of the abilities and skills of its individual members.

The team charter

Once your team is selected – either by chance, circumstance, yourself or others – then it's time for you, the team leader, to bring them together.

But this first meeting isn't just a social, 'getting-to-know-you', event. It's the beginning of the process by which this collection of individuals will evolve, change and develop into an effective, working, results-generating team. It may also be the first time that you meet them in your role of team leader. There should be no exemptions from this meeting – it's a must-be-there meeting for all the team members and should be scheduled and arranged in ways that recognize that.

The primary purpose of this meeting is the generation, discussion and agreement of the Team Charter.

Insight

Creating and agreeing a Team Charter is your first step towards becoming a team.

This isn't a legal contract or agreement. In fact, for some teams it won't even exist on paper. But, nevertheless, it is important. This is because it identifies the why, what, when and how of the team. It will provide the answers to the obvious questions of 'What are we going to do?', 'How long will it take?' and 'Who are our customers?' It will also answer the more subtle – but just as important – questions such as 'How are we going to work together?', 'Will we all be involved in key decisions?' and 'What principles are important to us as a team?' The answers to these and other questions make up the Team Charter. They need to be hammered out in this first meeting. It does help if you, as team leader, have thought through where you stand on the key issues and prepared a draft document for discussion. This should tell the team about:

- *its task*
  - ▷ *what, by when, at what cost, etc.*
- *the key customers*
  - ▷ *names, roles, expectations*
- *the project stakeholders*
  - ▷ *names, expectations, conflicts.*

It should also give them some idea of the options for:

- *how communications are to be managed*
  - *with customers and stakeholders and between team members*
- *how team performance will be measured*
  - *key results, milestones, outcomes*
- *what procedures and rules will be used*
  - *must-be-done rules, areas of discretion*
- *how the team will work together*
  - *principles of team operations.*

Remember that this is a draft and try and get the level of detail right. Too much and people will feel that any real discussion has been pre-empted; too little and the discussions will produce nothing more than a series of 'broad-brush' generalities. It's worth starting off with a package of statements which define, irrespective of the detail level of your draft, the core principles of the way in which you want the team to operate. Good examples would be:

- *Working together is more productive than working apart.*
- *Joint decisions are stronger than solo ones.*
- *Team meetings are jointly owned.*

In the end, the content, detail, form and structure of your Team Charter is down to you and your team. But if it's going to work then it must provide urgency and direction to the team's efforts as well as being a means of focusing the creativity and energy of all team members.

Team building

We've already seen that the first team meeting is important – if not vital – to the creation of the Team Charter. But that's not all that happens there – it's also the beginning of the team building process.

But teams don't just spring spontaneously into existence at that first meeting. The process of team growth and change is one that develops gradually. It takes time for the team to complete the journey from a collection of individuals to a cohesive, supportive, flexible and productive team. To do that they have to change, develop and grow. It's a journey that takes them from the inhibited watchfulness of their first meetings, through conflict and the development of their own 'home-grown' set of rules and standards to, finally, become a team. One of the more accessible views about how this happens tells us that a team 'grows' through four stages called 'forming', 'storming', 'norming' and 'performing' (Figure 6.2). This process needs help and support, which is what team building is about.

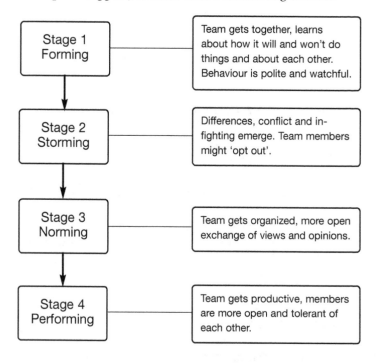

Figure 6.2 Steps and stages of team development.

At this point, it's important to realize that the route that each team follows on this journey is unique to that team. It has to be, since that team itself is unique. But despite this uniqueness there are some basic factors that are common and important. One of these is about spending a lot of time together, even to the point of working in the same office or suite of offices. A lot of what happens in the team development process is informal. It's about getting to know each other, getting to know and respect each other's strengths and weaknesses, finding ways of working together. There often isn't time for this to take place outside the day-to-day operations of the project, it's a do-it-as-we-go process. It's also a process that takes place better and more quickly when people are in close proximity to each other. Walls and doors get in the way. In large teams this will mean dedicated space for the full-time staff. In small teams or teams with part-time members this means a dedicated 'team room' to which team members come to work on the team task and in which work-in-progress is left.

Another important element of building your team is the way in which conflict is handled.

Insight

Real teams start to emerge when the people in them start to take risks – about things like conflict, trust and dependence.

Conflict is necessary to the process of becoming a real team. It occurs because people don't get on with each other, because people have different attitudes or sets of values and because people have different expectations. But most of all, in real teams, it occurs because all of the team are committed to doing their best for the team. Dealing with it isn't always easy; often feelings run high and voices are raised. But dealing with it is a must. If you sit on it, ignore it, push it under the surface of day-to-day relations, then it'll just resurface elsewhere – and be the worse for it! If you're going to deal with it effectively then you may have to change the way that you think about it. It has to become a constructive opportunity rather than something to be endured.

The key factors in dealing with conflict are communication, communication and communication.

Frank, open talking and real listening are risky. But they are essential if you're going to have a real team. Taking the risk to be open in conflict can, on the down-side, lead to hurt feelings, hostility, enmity – even hatred. The up-side, though, is the hard-won mutual trust and interdependence that's essential to a real team.

Project teams

On the face of it, the task of creating a project team and then getting it to work doesn't appear to be a difficult one. After all, the sorts of people who are attracted to projects usually have that extra 'get up and go' that a project needs and one of the skills of good management is said to be that of 'recruiting good people and then letting them get on with it'.

But it isn't as simple as that – because project teams are different. Like the project itself, project teams are one-off. They are collections of people who come together for a defined and limited period of time. They do so in order to create a unique project outcome. These people may be part- or full-time members of the team and they will only be in that team for as long as their particular skills and knowledge are needed by the project. These factors generate a set of stresses that are particular to project teams. The result is that, in addition to the basic entry and team role criteria that were identified earlier in this chapter (see pages 117 onwards), we need project team members to have additional skills to cope with the stresses and strains of the project.

These are:

▶ *higher than average functional skills*
▶ *sensitivity to the 'politics' of the project*

- ▶ *strong problem-solving skills*
- ▶ *a willingness to share both successes and mistakes – and then move on to the next target.*

The compositions of project teams often reflect the nature of the project outcome. For example, the team on a new office block project will contain civil engineers, structural engineers, electrical engineers and heating and ventilation specialists while the team for the production of a new book will involve a production editor, a graphic designer, a cost accountant, a printer, sales personnel and a marketing person. But if the people with these specialist skills are going to become a team then not only do they need to have the skills we identified earlier, they also need a project manager who is able to gain their trust and communicate with them. Inexperienced project managers often feel that in order to achieve this they need to know as much as the specialists in their team.

But this is not so. Indeed, there is a saying amongst NASA project staff that a project manager who acts as if he is his own specialist staff would probably try to do open heart surgery on himself (or herself)! In other words, it isn't necessary or sensible for the project manager to be as good a specialist as they are. What is necessary and sensible is that the project manager can ask these specialists the 'right' questions and, more importantly, understand the answers.

Insight

Good effective project teamwork starts to happen when you all move from 'me' to 'we'.

Good project teams are rare animals. We often have project teams made up of people who are good at their job. They are good structural engineers, clever piping engineers or excellent social workers, nurses or administrators – or even, for family projects, just good at being a member of a family. But we rarely have project teams of people who are good at their job and good at being a team member. Yet the value of a balanced and integrated project team is one that cannot be understated. A project team like that – a project team that works – can overcome overwhelming difficulties, trials and tribulations and bring the project to a successful conclusion.

Use the following questionnaire to check out your project team.

Project team checkout

Under each of the headings below ring a number which is nearest to the way that your project team operates – and then add up your total.

	Definitely applies to us	Applies to us	Not sure	Does not apply to us	Definitely doesn't apply to us
1 Process and size					
We come together easily and frequently.	5	4	3	2	1
Our discussions are open and interactive.	5	4	3	2	1
Everybody is involved in what goes on.	5	4	3	2	1
We have enough people.	5	4	3	2	1
2 Goal and targets					
We all know what we are trying to achieve.	5	4	3	2	1
We all know how our performance will be measured.	5	4	3	2	1
Our goals are realistic.	5	4	3	2	1

	Definitely applies to us	Applies to us	Not sure	Does not apply to us	Definitely doesn't apply to us
3 Skills					
We have all the functional skills that we need.	5	4	3	2	1
We spend time developing new skills.	5	4	3	2	1
Our decisions involve us all.	5	4	3	2	1
We use conflict constructively.	5	4	3	2	1
4 Working approach					
The way we work draws on the skills and experience of all team members.	5	4	3	2	1
We solve problems in fact-based ways.	5	4	3	2	1
We can change the way we work.	5	4	3	2	1

Key   **Total**

14–42	This seems to be more like a group than a team.
43–56	Good – check your scores with the rest of the team and use the results to focus your joint efforts to improve.
57–70	See if the rest of the team agree with your scores. If they do you are either a top-class team or all suffering from terminal group think.

What next?

Now you can move on to read about how to manage and control that most essential of project ingredients – money. But, before you do that, read through the following list – this chapter's ten most important messages.

TOP TEN MESSAGES

1 *A team is a social group – rarely more than ten people – who work cooperatively.*

2 *The people in this team will have shared objectives.*

3 *Good teams are about change – they make things happen.*

4 *They also work in ways that out-perform not only the sum of their member's individual efforts but also the efforts of all other sorts of social group.*

5 *You should have people in your team because of their functional skills and their ability to work co-operatively with others.*

6 *You should, however, also make sure that they are able to carry out the required team roles.*

7 *Building your team starts with the generation of a joint Team Charter and continues when the team spends time together and goes through the Forming, Storming, Norming and Performing stages.*

8 *Project teams are different; they consist of collections of people who come together for a defined and limited period of time in order to create a unique project outcome.*

9 *Project team members can be part or full time and will only be in that team for as long as their particular skills and knowledge are needed.*

10 *Successful project teams have members with:*
- ▷ *higher than average functional skills*
- ▷ *sensitivity to the 'politics' of both the project and its parent organization*
- ▷ *strong problem-solving skills*
- ▷ *a willingness to share both successes and mistakes – and then move on to the next target.*

7

Managing your project money

In this chapter you will learn:
- *How to estimate your project's money needs*
- *What factors to take into account when budgeting*

Money, money and money

In order to achieve our project's outcomes we must spend money. There are few, if any, exceptions to this rule. Indeed, money is so important to the project that its effective management is one of the must-do, must-have factors of successful project management. There are rules and procedures to help us in this management. These are usually grouped under the headings of Cost Accounting or Financial Project Management. We met some of these in Chapter 2 when we saw how financial ratios such as the project's 'rate of return', 'net present value' and 'profitability index' are used to help choose which project to implement.

However, the objective of this chapter is not to convert you into a cost accountant or even to make you over into a financial manager. It is to provide you with a basic understanding of the ways and means of your project money. This understanding starts, in this chapter, by looking at the ways in which your project's money needs are estimated. It continues in Chapter 8 when we look at the ways that money is monitored and controlled. Once you have acquired that knowledge, you'll have taken a significant step towards being able to manage your project effectively.

Cost, cost and more cost

Cost is the commonest word in the accountant's lexicon. But it rarely appears on its own. For that reason we need to look more closely at it and the ways in which it is used in our projects.

A cost, in the accounting sense, is something that springs into being when we spend money or anticipate that we will spend it. This happens when we buy our project materials – such as bricks or wood – or when we pay people for work that they have done on the project or rent machines to use on that project. The conventions of accounting tell us that these are called **material costs**, **labour costs** and **equipment costs** respectively. But costs can also be **direct**, as when we charge them directly to a specific project activity, or **indirect**, as when we allow them to be absorbed in the overall costs of the project. These indirect costs are also often called overheads.

But these aren't the only ways that we describe costs. For our project costs can also be described as being **fixed**, as when they remain at the same level irrespective of the project workload, or **variable**, as when they vary with the rate of activity or project workload. The costs of our project also include the **standard** cost. This is a predetermined cost which is used, initially, to estimate the overall cost of a project activity and, later, to monitor the cost performance of the project. It is generated from historic data and can be calculated for any activity or resource in the project. We can have, for example, a standard cost for laying bricks and a standard cost for the bricks themselves. Both would be in Rand, £ or $ per 1,000 bricks.

> **Insight**
> 'Always count the cost.' (American proverb)

The predicted sum of all these costs is the project's total cost estimate. This, as we saw in Chapter 1, is one of those key features whose dimensions define the boundaries of the project.

This predicted cost of a project can also exert a considerable influence upon whether that project is chosen – as we saw in Chapter 2. Later (in Chapter 8) we will see its role in the monitoring and controlling of the achieved or actual cost of a project.

What we need to do now is to look at how this predicted total cost is generated.

Hunches, guesstimates and estimates

Making sure that we have enough money to answer our project's needs isn't just important – it's essential.

But doing that is not one of those retrospective, after-the-spend, actions, nor is it a crystal ball based process designed to pluck arbitrary future figures out of the air. To answer our project's money needs we need to be able to predict accurately not only how much money is needed but also when it is needed.

The project estimate is the first step towards that knowledge.

This estimate is used in a number of ways. It can help us, for example, in the very early days of the project, to answer such questions as 'Is this new product worth further investigation?' or 'Is this book worth publishing?' It is also used in the process of deciding which of a number of competing projects represents the best investment for the funds of the organization or our personal money. Finally, once our project has been approved, this estimate becomes the core of the project's budget. That budget is used in the process of monitoring and controlling the project – in which actual spend is measured and then compared to the benchmark data of the estimate.

But each of these tasks has different needs. For example, to find out whether the idea of a project is worth further investigation we need an initial cost estimate with a low level of accuracy. But when we come to decide if we want to release the money that the project needs, then we need a higher level of accuracy for our cost estimate. But, whatever their accuracy levels, it is important that these estimates are generated by the exercise of skill and judgement and using the best available data sources.

Doing that is not an exercise in risk taking or intuition. It is a logical exercise that is based on the best available information about:

- ▶ *the intended outcome of the project*
- ▶ *the activities needed to achieve that outcome*
- ▶ *the costs of those or similar activities.*

However, the level of detail and accuracy of the available information varies throughout the project's life cycle. In the Feasibility phase we have little detailed information. We may, for example, only have an approximate idea of the size, weight, output or floor area of our project's outcomes. This means that the estimate that we generate is based on a generalized 'broad brush' outcome definition, such as 'a four-seat family car' or 'a portable computer'. As such, it has a low level of accuracy. This sort of estimate is often used as a 'toe in the water' aimed at finding out whether it's worth exploring the project further. Its accuracy can be as low as ± 50%. The names given to this sort of estimate reflect this, such as a 'seat of the pants' estimate, or a 'ball-park' estimate or even an 'order of magnitude' estimate. Their use for any other purpose than very preliminary decision taking is not advised.

Insight

A minimum of information is used to develop this type of 'Ball Park' estimate. The estimate is often generated by using data from similar past projects.

By the end of the Feasibility phase of the project's life cycle a go/no go decision will have been made about the project. To do this we need an estimate with a higher level of accuracy – usually ± 10%. To generate this we need more detail about our project outcome and the time-line of its generation. This detail is generated in two stages. These lead, respectively, to the Budget estimate and the

Sanction estimate. The first of these, the Budget estimate, has an accuracy level of ± 20%. For projects with high cost levels or high levels of risk, the Budget estimate is based on preliminary design work. In smaller, less complex or lower risk projects this design work is very limited and the Budget estimate might even be based on comparisons with other similar projects. This estimate, which is also called a Preliminary, Predesign or Feasibility estimate, is used to help us decide whether – or not – to start the detailed design of the project's outcome. This detailed design work is used to generate the second estimate – the Sanction estimate. With an accuracy level of ± 10% the Sanction estimate is used to decide whether – or not – to proceed with the project. It also provides a foundation for the final estimate – the Definitive or Project Control estimate.

Insight

In a Project Control estimate we price each and every item in a thorough manner.

This is only generated when the design work for the project outcome has been frozen – a step which, as we saw in Chapter 3, enables us to create our project specification. It has an accuracy level of ± 5 to 10% and, as we will see later in Chapter 8, provides the benchmark for the monitoring and controlling of the project.

All of these estimates of the project's potential future cost are based on the information that is available at the time of their generation.

Information, data, facts and figures

Given the importance of our project cost estimates it seems almost too obvious that we should use the best information that we can get to generate them. For most of us, however, the problem lies not in that information itself – but in where to find it.

When we generate our initial cost estimate we often only have a broad statement of intent about the project's outcome. This might tell us, for example, that the project is about creating a chemical plant to manufacture ammonia at the rate of 500 metric tons/day, installing a drinks vending machine in an office block or taking a holiday in Hawaii. But, limited as this information is, it gets us started. For, by using the records of previous similar projects, indicative costs quoted by manufacturers or a friend's memory of the cost of his or her holiday, we can generate a 'ball-park' or an 'order of magnitude' estimate of the project's likely cost.

But if we are to increase the accuracy of our estimate then we need more information – information about the activities to be undertaken and resources needed to support those activities and, most importantly, their anticipated costs. The first of these, the activity information, is important. For without it we may find that the cost estimate for our project for the installation of a drinks vending machine doesn't include the cost of providing drainage of waste water and spillages away from the machine or even the cost of providing sufficient electrical power for the machine's safe operation. One way of avoiding this sort of situation is to sit down and generate a list. This should cover, firstly, the areas in which work is needed and secondly, the actual work that is needed. An example of the first sort of list – which is often called a Work Breakdown Schedule (WBS) – is given in Figure 7.1.

Vending Machine Project
Work Breakdown Schedule

Phase 1: Activity areas

Supply machine
Selection of location
Provision of electrical power
Provision of potable water
Provision of waste water drainage
Provision of storage for consumables
Provision of solid waste facilities – cups etc.

Figure 7.1 Example of Phase 1 of a Work Breakdown Schedule.

On a small project – such as our vending machine project – this may be all that you need to do. Once you have decided which machine to buy and where the machine and its storage facilities are to be located then you can use this list as a check-list when you get contractors to provide quotations for each or all of the other separate activities.

Insight

The WBS helps you to convert hundreds or thousands of tasks into understandable chunks.

On larger projects, life is more complicated and your WBS will need to have several levels – each with ascending degrees of detail – for each of the types of estimate that we identified earlier in this chapter. This process goes on until you reach the final and definitive version of this WBS – that contained in the project specification.

The data that we use to generate the costs contained in each of these levels of estimate comes from a variety of sources. These can include:

▶ *web sites*
▶ *previous projects*
▶ *suppliers*
▶ *contractors*
▶ *cost engineering consultants*
▶ *trade and government cost indices*
▶ *trade magazines*
▶ *professional journals and publications*
▶ *reference and textbooks.*

However, you must remember that, however good these sources are, in the end the accuracy of your estimate lies in your hands. If you miss something important out or add something unnecessary in, then it could make the difference between the success or failure of your project.

Insight

The best cost estimates come together when you use both the best information available and your own judgement.

Top-down or bottom-up

The methods that we use to generate estimates will change with the level of accuracy required.

In the early part of the project life cycle – when levels of accuracy as low as ± 50% are acceptable – 'top-down' methods can be used. These, as we will soon see, start either from the size of the project outcome or from the cost of a major part of that outcome. In the later stages – when levels of accuracy as high as ± 5–10% are needed – 'bottom-up' methods are used. These are much more detailed and often start from the detail of individual work items.

Top-down

Top-down estimating methods start from information that contains the lowest level of detail about the project. This can be either a statement about the size of the project – as in a 200,000 m² warehouse, a 200-page book, 100 t/day ammonia plant or a 14-day holiday in Hawaii – or the size and cost of its most significant item.

When we use the size of the project outcome to generate our cost estimate we use the exponential method. The cost estimate for the new project is generated by multiplying the known cost of a completed similar project by the ratio of the size of new outcome to the size of the completed project's outcome raised to a given power – or exponent. When you express this as an equation it looks like this:

Cost of new project $= $ Cost of old project $\times (S_{new}/S_{old})^{0.66}$

Where S_{new} $=$ size or capacity of your new project

S_{old} $=$ size or capacity of old project

Complicated? No, not really, as you'll see from the following example:

Let's say that we want to estimate the cost of building a warehouse with a floor area of 200,000 m². An identical warehouse with a floor area of 150,000 m², completed last month, had a total material and erection cost of, say, £250,000. We can estimate that the cost of the new, larger, warehouse will be:

$$£250,000 \times (200,000/150,000)^{0.66}$$

or   £302,273

If we had ratioed these costs in direct proportion to the size of the warehouses we would have estimated the cost as:

$$£250,000 \times (200,000/150,000)$$

or   £333,333 – which is over 10% more!

The exponents used depend, to some extent, on the nature of your project. In most situations an exponent in the range of 0.6 to 0.75 is acceptable but there is some evidence that software projects require an exponent which is as high as 1.20. When you are using this method you need to:

▶ *take care to ensure that you are comparing like with like*
▶ *remember that the accuracy of the result is as low as ± 50%.*

The second of the top-down methods that we can use is called the factorial or parametric estimating method. This method of cost estimation starts from a detailed and accurate cost for a core item in the project outcome – such as a boiler in a boiler house project, a vending machine in a drinks vending machine project or the hotel costs for a 14-day holiday in Hawaii. This core cost is then used to find the cost of the other bits of the project – such as piping, electrical services, airline flights, etc. For example, if we know that the cost of the vending machine is £2,000 then, by the use of factors, we can estimate that the cost of the water supply might be

($£2,000 \times 0.12$) = $£240$ and the cost of the electrical services might be ($£2,000 \times 0.08$) = $£160$. When we add together all of these costs, we arrive at the cost estimate for the project. There are a number of sources of the factors and when you are using this method you need to be sure that:

▶ *the factors are developed from a data base that is relevant, accurate and large enough*
▶ *the project outcome is scalable.*

Bottom-up

Insight

Bottom-up estimates are built up from the most detailed WBS level available and aggregated to give totals for the project as a whole. They are the opposite of top-down estimates.

Bottom-up estimating starts from the information contained in the project's Work Breakdown Schedule (WBS). The greater the detail in this schedule, the higher the level of accuracy of the estimate. As we saw earlier the highest level of WBS detail exists in its final and definitive version contained in the project specification. The most accurate bottom-up estimates use this level of the WBS to estimate the cost of individual work items. These are then accumulated into the total cost of the project. On most projects this involves a lot of work – and work costs money – so the project manager will need to weigh the cost of generating such an estimate against the value of its accuracy.

Whatever the level of accuracy we choose, the information about the individual work items that we use has to be both realistic and well founded. For example, none of our project work starts with instantly high levels of activity. Like all human activities their work rates start low, rise, stabilize and then fall, to cease at the completion of the work item. These differing work rates will obviously influence either the resources, such as labour, that we need for the task or, if that is limited, the time taken to complete the task.

We'll look at this in more detail. Let's assume that we need a total of 600 person hours to paint the interior of a new office block and that the project schedule says that this has to be completed in three 40-hour working weeks. If we divide the people hours by the hours available, i.e. $(600/(40 \times 3))$, this tells us that we need five people. But this apparently logical calculation ignores the fact that work rates start low, rise, and then fall. One way of allowing for these varying rates is to assume that the initial low, but rising, work-rate phase lasts for a fifth of the total calendar time available, i.e. 24 hours or three eight-hour days, and that the run-down phase at the end lasts for 30% of that total calendar time, i.e. 36 hours or four and a half eight-hour working days. The peak activity level will take place over the seven and a half eight-hour days between these phases. If we average the rate at which work takes place during both the initial and final phases of the task then we can calculate that:

$$\text{Number of people} = \frac{600 \text{ people hours}}{(3 + 4.5) \text{ days at 4 hours per day}}$$
$$\text{equivalent} + 7.5 \text{ days at 8 hours per day}$$

Number of people = 600/90 = 6.66 people

Remember that if we had assumed a constant activity rate throughout the whole of this 15-day period then our estimate of the number of people required would have been five – which is a third too low!

Below and above the line

We have already seen that the costs that make up our estimates can be described in various ways.

These include labour and material costs that can be direct or indirect depending on whether they are directly charged to a particular project activity or to the overall business of running the project. An example of an indirect labour cost would be the salary costs of the project manager, secretaries, clerks etc. An example of a direct material cost would be the bricks, concrete, sand, wood, glass, tiles, etc. that are used in an office block project.

But we also may need equipment to complete the tasks that are demanded by our project. This equipment can be the scaffolding that we need to access the roof of our office block, the computers that we use to schedule and monitor our project or the suitcases that we need for our holiday in Hawaii. This equipment can be hired, leased or bought. But, however they are acquired, the cost of doing so needs to be included in your project cost estimate. All of these are called, in accounting terms, 'above-the-line' costs.

There is another, just as important, group of costs that are called 'below-the-line' costs. Amongst these are the costs that accountants usually group under the collective title of 'miscellaneous fees'. These indirect or overhead costs can include design charges from outside agencies, consultancy fees, inspection fees, the costs of insuring against claims for loss and damage from other people, tax liability and our holiday insurance against illness, cancellation, etc.

These 'below-the-line' costs also include an allowance for inflation. You will remember, from Chapter 2, that the Net Present Value method of assessing a project proposal took account of the fact that the value of our money changes with time. If the life span of our project exceeds six months then we need to protect ourselves against the effects of this change. We do this by including an inflation allowance in our cost estimate – as a below-the-line cost. The inflation rate used to calculate this allowance comes from government and industry predictions. On projects with a long time-span, this inflation can be covered by a cost review clause that allows for the sanctioning of additional funds if inflation indices exceed a defined level.

Generating an estimate is a complicated task and one that, by its nature, attempts to anticipate the future costs of events. Obviously, there are risks in doing that and a project manager can find himself or herself hostage to tomorrow's fortunes. This can come about for a number of reasons. Mistakes are made, information and costs are left out of the estimate, currency exchange rates change, new technology becomes available or earthquakes, hurricanes or strikes happen. What our estimate needs is a below-the-line sum that covers for these eventualities. This is called a contingency allowance.

The contingency allowance has a typical value of around 5% of the total project estimate. But it is not intended to cover for changes in project scope or for failures in the estimating process. It is intended to act as a hedge against unknown or difficult-to-predict events. Its value for your project will be influenced by things like the risk level or novelty of the project (see Chapter 2) and an assessment of the real likelihood of events such as earthquakes, hurricanes or strikes. Finally, use the Project Estimate Checkout below to make sure that you've covered all that you need to cover in your estimate.

Project estimate checkout

Does your project estimate include:

1 Overheads such as:
- ▷ design fees?
- ▷ consultancy fees?
- ▷ insurance costs?

2 Labour costs such as:
- ▷ project manager/team costs?
- ▷ direct labour costs?
- ▷ sub-contract labour costs?
- ▷ temporary labour cost?

(Contd)

3 Material costs such as those needed for:
  ▷ services supply, such as electricity, water, gas heating and ventilation?
  ▷ any building work?
  ▷ special materials such as:
    – optical fibre network?
    – pre-recorded training videos?

4 Equipment costs such as:
  ▷ purchase?
  ▷ lease?
  ▷ rental?

5 Contingency allowance?

6 Inflation allowance?

Budgets

The point at which our estimate changes into our budget is a significant one for the project. It is one of those project milestones, one of those significant points that mark a major change in the pace or rhythm of the project.

It usually occurs around the point at which the project's money is sanctioned. The shift from being an estimate to becoming a budget results in two significant changes in the information that is so vital to the financial well-being of our budget.

The first of these lies in the fact that the budget tells us not only what is to be spent – as the estimate did – it also tells us when that expenditure is to take place. The estimate that we have brought together now becomes a time-based statement of our financial intent, one in which the sequence of our expenditure from the beginning to the end of the project is defined. To do this the budget draws heavily on the content of the project plan. This, as we saw in Chapter 4, tells us about the starts, finishes and resource demands of our project's activities. The relationship between project plan and project budget is a close one (see Figure 7.2). So close that it provides us with one of the mechanisms by which we can 'fine-tune' our management of the project.

The second of these changes is just as important. For with that shift – from estimate to budget – and the sanction process that accompanies it, this financial information changes from being an expression of our intent, a forecast or a prediction, to becoming a limit of what we can spend in our project. This is a significant change. It means that our project budget not only tells us when our expenditure is to take place, it now also tells us what the limit or boundary of that expenditure is to be. Our project's budget provides a baseline, a datum level, against which we can measure, monitor and control our project expenditure. This is what we look at in the next chapter.

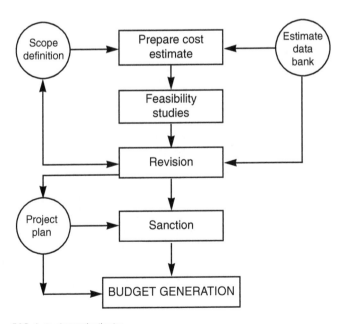

Figure 7.2 Budgets, plans and estimates.

What next?

In the next chapter you'll look at ways in which a project's progress can be monitored and controlled and find out that the way that you do that monitoring and controlling can contribute to the project's success. But, before you do that, read through the following list – this chapter's ten most important messages.

TOP TEN MESSAGES

1 *A project's money starts with an estimate.*

2 *Creating an accurate estimate is vital to the success of your project.*

3 *A project estimate is based on the available information about the project outcome and the activities needed to achieve that outcome.*

4 *That estimate will also take into account the historic costs of identical or similar activities.*

5 *The types of estimate are:*
> ▷ *ball park, seat of the pants, order of magnitude estimate (± 50%)*
> ▷ *budget, predesign, feasibility estimate (± 20%)*
> ▷ *sanction estimate (± 10%)*
> ▷ *definitive estimate (± 5–10%).*

6 *Top-down estimates use exponential or factorial estimating techniques.*

7 *Bottom-up estimates use costs generated from Work Breakdown Schedule (WBS) data by use of labour, material and equipment costs.*

8 *All estimates involve additional 'below-the-line' costs such as insurance and tax charges and allowances for inflation and contingencies.*

9 *An estimate becomes a budget when a project is sanctioned.*

10 *A project budget contains information about:*
> ▷ *how much money is to be spent*
> ▷ *on what that money is to be spent*
> ▷ *when it is to be spent.*

8

Monitoring and controlling
your project

In this chapter you will learn:
- *How to control your project*
- *How to measure and monitor your project's progress with reference to its goals and targets*

Full steam ahead

Once your project is under way, the pace of its activity increases rapidly. Statements of future intent become matters of everyday reality. The brave prospects of forward-looking plans become, first, reality and then, finally, history. With all this change and progress there also comes, inevitably, the erosive drift of time. Risks that we had thought remote become real and distinct possibilities, some even evolving into present certainties.

The nature of these difficulties can be as various as the flowers in spring. For example, important material deliveries can be delayed, vital equipment breaks down, key personnel can go sick or be re-assigned to other projects or new technology fails to deliver. It can snow, rain or hail in summer, Head Office can put a freeze on all project spending and our children can catch measles on the eve of our holiday departure.

But not all of our difficulties are as major or as serious as these. More often, the problems of our projects consist of a multitude of apparently minor, trivial incidents. But these incidents can still be significant. For their effects, small as they may be, can nevertheless accumulate to significant levels and then cause delays, cost overruns and shortfalls in outcome performance or quality. The reasons for and causes of these deviations from our plan are also various. They can come about because we fail to plan with adequate foresight or because we ignore or discount real risks or, most human of all, because we make mistakes.

In short, things don't always happen the way that we planned that they would.

Insight

'Life is what happens to you while you're busy making other plans.' (John Lennon)

This sort of situation crops up on almost every project. Very, very few projects are exempt and coping with it is one of the key skills shown by experienced project managers. But when these drifts and deviations occur, what is important is not that they happen – since they are largely history by the time we become aware of them – but the ways that we respond to them. For if that response is to be effective, if it is to protect and maintain our ability to create the outcomes of our project at the scheduled time with the desired performance at the right cost, then our response must contain two vital elements.

The first of these is contained in the ways in which we identify and react to these differences between what we planned and what we have been able to achieve. These are rooted in the tools that we use to identify, define and solve our projects' problems. These we will look at in the next chapter (Chapter 9).

The second of these vital elements is discussed in this chapter. This is about the ways and means that we use, firstly, to tell us when the activities of our project are not as they ought to be and, secondly, to correct or limit the effects of those deviations from our project plan. In short, this chapter is about the ways in which we monitor and control our projects.

Monitoring

When we monitor something, we observe, measure or test it.

Let's assume, for example, that we want to monitor the hours of sunshine in Tucson, Arizona, or the amount of rain that falls in Liverpool, England. The first thing that we need to do is to find a way of measuring this sunshine or rainfall. But not just any old way will do; it needs to be a way that is reliable, accurate, economic and repeatable. Once we have found this then we can start to measure the sunshine or rainfall – probably on a daily basis. The daily data that we generate needs to be recorded. Those records need to be organized so that we can, for instance, compare month with month or year with year. We might also want to analyse this data in ways that tell us about long-term trends, patterns or other effects. Other people might also be interested in the results of all this activity. Because of this, the ways in which we record and express these records of sunshine or rainfall need to be both accessible and understandable.

Insight

Trying to monitor the progress of your project when you don't have a means of measurement or a performance standard is rather like setting out on a cross-country trip in a car without a fuel gauge.

The ways in which we monitor the progress of our projects are similar. But instead of providing us with passive numbers, our project monitoring provides us with active information; information such as the answers to such questions as 'Is this activity on schedule?', 'Have we overspent the project budget?' or 'What is the project's probable finish date?'. They tell us whether our project is – or isn't – on plan. But that's not all that our project monitoring tells us. We need to know about the where and when of our project's drifts and deviations. For, unlike our monitoring of Tucson's sunshine or Liverpool's rainfall, the results of this monitoring lead us on to another vital element in the management of our project – that of controlling it. Once we have the answers to our questions then we can begin to do something about the cause of these differences – and thus bring the project back 'on course'.

Project monitoring – what and when

The effective monitoring of our project is important. It tells us where we are. From that we can predict where we are likely to be in the future. Then we can work out what we need to do to influence or change that future. It also provides us with the sort of performance measurement that we can use to motivate our project team.

But this monitoring cannot be an indiscriminate across-the-board activity. That would give us far too much data and too little time to analyse or react to it. Our project monitoring needs to be focused so that its contribution to our projects is not only relevant, it's also timely and maximized.

The first step that we take towards that goal is to decide:

▶ *what we are going to monitor*
▶ *how often we are going to monitor it.*

The choice of what we monitor is one that must be made with care. For if we monitor too few things or things that are unimportant then we might miss the drift or movement of a key aspect and not be able to react until it is too late. If we monitor too many things, then we finish up with too much data and not enough time to analyse it properly. What we monitor must also be related to the key features of our project – Cost, Performance and Time. The closer that relationship is, the better the result. But that's not all that we must consider. For if what we monitor is going to help us manage our project then not only must it be related to those key features, it must also be, in itself, significant, believable and easy to measure and understand.

Insight
'What gets measured gets done.' (Tom Peters)

Finding project 'pulse-points' that meet these criteria isn't always easy – but it can be done. For example, in a project to write a new book we can monitor the number of words written, and in a project to redecorate a room we can monitor the wall area repainted or re-papered. Don't forget that you can also monitor how things are going by that well-known technique of 'management-by-walking-about'. There's no real substitute for getting out there, actually seeing what is happening and talking to the people involved. A decision 'on the ground' can be the proverbial 'stitch in time that saves nine'.

Of course, even these 'pulse-point' measurements don't tell us the whole story. To gain that, we need to be able to link them back to those two core sources of project information – the project plan and the project budget. Both of these provide us with information that will help us to decide the other key aspect of our monitoring – when or how often we do it.

Deciding the 'right' frequency of our monitoring measurements is as important as deciding what to monitor. Too often and we drown in data, not often enough and we miss the early drift that leads to later major deviations. Getting it right depends on things like the overall length of the project and its risk level. For example, on most long projects, measurement and reporting on a weekly frequency would be sufficient. On short projects – in which the events of a single day can be crucial – measurement and reporting on a daily or even half daily frequency would be warranted. High-risk projects demand, for obvious reasons, more frequent measurements than low-risk projects. Whatever you decide is right for you, remember that in this – as in other areas – regularity is important. Regular monitoring keeps us in touch with our project and that enables us to manage it successfully, as Figure 8.1 below tells us.

THE PROJECT ORGANIZATION FRAMEWORK

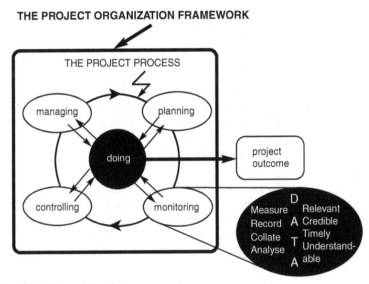

Figure 8.1 Monitoring and the project process.

The project plan and monitoring

When we first create our project plan it is about our intended future actions. At that time its value lies in the ways that it helps us to estimate both the cost and duration of the project. But once our project gets under way that changes. For then our plan becomes a road map for our journey, a 'this-is-what-you-do-next' guide for our actions.

Insight
Monitoring project progress against the project plan should be a routine, rather than an occasional, activity.

But that isn't all that it does for us. For we can also use that plan to monitor the progress of our project. When we do this the plan will tell us whether its activities are up to, behind, or ahead of schedule. If we find that they are behind schedule then we need to decide what we are going to do about that. The project plan can act as a framework within which we evaluate the options for decisions that we must then make. We can use it as a base-line from which we can develop hybrid or alternative plans. This will help us to see the results of our 'what if we...?' proposals and test the feasibility of our options. To do this our plans must be, as we saw in Chapter 4, clear, unambiguous, easily understood and, above all, capable of change. Changing our project plan is also one of the ways in which we control our project, as we shall see later in this chapter. But if that change is to be effective then it must always be preceded by and based on the data generated by the process of monitoring.

We also saw in Chapter 4 that most information is best presented in a graphic visual form. The use of the project plan for monitoring is no exception to this. The filled-in bars of the Gantt chart tell us about the progress of our activities. But numbers also have their place in this process and we can represent our progress and compare it to our targets by the data recorded on the nodes and arrows of the AOA networks or the nodes of our Precedence networks.

Milestones

One of the most common ways of monitoring the progress of our project uses milestones.

Insight

A project milestone, by definition, has zero duration and demands no effort – but does give you the opportunity to validate the current state of your project.

These, like the milestones of our highways, can be used to mark the stages of our project's journey from start to completion. They are best set at the end or beginning of an activity – for ease of identification – and are usually limited to Critical Path activities. On a Gantt chart they can be indicated graphically by an icon such as a diamond (◊). The unfilled ◊ represents a scheduled milestone and the filled ♦, a completed milestone. Our progress towards their achievement can also be reported in the words and dates of a milestone report that contains such information as shown in Figure 8.2.

Milestone no.	Scheduled date	Anticipated date	Achieved date	Notes
4	25th Oct.	–	24th Oct.	Completed ahead of schedule
5	13th Dec.	15th Dec.	–	Material delivery delay anticipated

Figure 8.2 Milestones report example.

The milestones of our projects tell us, as on our highways and roads, how far we have travelled. But they are not the only tool that we can use to monitor the status of our projects.

Limits

We can also find out how our projects are progressing by using Limit Testing.

Insight

A Limit Test enables you to perform pass/fail testing using upper and lower limits that you specify.

This involves comparing the current value of, say, project milestone achievement, to the value that we had planned. If there is a difference, then we need to know more about it. The larger the difference is, the quicker we need to know about it and the more detail we require. This technique can also, with a little imagination, be applied to other critical aspects of the project such as activity rates or project spend. Its advantages include its compatibility with most project management information systems (PMIS) and the ease of its operation.

The responses and actions that are triggered by a difference – between planned and achieved – need to be relevant to its size. For example, a milestone achievement rate that is 5% low will initiate an investigation, whereas a 10% underachievement would cause tighter control procedures to be initiated and higher frequencies of reporting.

ABC analysis

Another technique that we can use to monitor our project is Pareto or ABC analysis.

Insight

Vilfredo Pareto observed that 80% of Italy's wealth was held by only 20% of the population.

Commonly used in inventory management, ABC analysis is based on the work of Vilfredo Pareto, a 19th-century Italian economist. Pareto identified the empirical relationship that is often called the 80–20 rule. When used to control inventories this identifies the 20% of stocks that are responsible for 80% of total inventory costs. These are called Class A items. In our project we can use this rule to identify the 20% of activities that are responsible for 80% of project labour costs or the 20% of materials that are responsible for 80% of the project's material costs. Once we know which these Class A activities or materials are then we can adjust our measurement and reporting routines to make sure that they are measured and monitored more frequently. We can also extend our use of the 80–20 rule so that it takes into account more than just cost. For, having identified the Class A items or activities of our spend we can then reclassify these in terms of their use on the project's Critical Path activities – and then readjust our monitoring and reporting accordingly. This way we monitor for those items and activities that are important in relation to two of our project's dimensions – Cost and Time.

It's also worth noting that both ABC analysis and Limit Testing can make major contributions to the management of another of the project's scarce resources – the project manager's time – since he or she is only involved when the pre-set limit has been exceeded or when critical items are delayed or overspent.

The project budget and monitoring

In Chapter 7 we saw that the budget tells us not only what is to be spent but also when that spend is to take place. This sequence of project expenditure is defined from the beginning to the end of the project.

This flow of cash must be monitored. If we fail to do that then we put at risk our ability to achieve the targets that we have set for our project; targets that are defined in terms of Cost, Time and Performance. We have already seen how Limit Testing and ABC analysis can help us with this monitoring. Another of the ways that we can use is what is often called the S curve, as illustrated in Figure 8.3.

What the S curve shows us are the trends in and differences between the project's budgeted, actual and predicted spend. But what it doesn't show us is the causes of the differences between the planned and actual spend – and these are important, as we shall soon see.

Let's assume that, as in the S curve shown above, the cumulative actual cost of our project is less than what we had planned – an apparently comfortable situation, you might think. But this

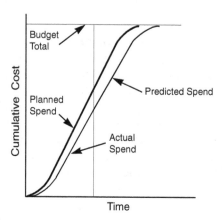

Figure 8.3 The S curve.

could have occurred because either the work completed was on schedule but cost less than we had planned or because the work completed was behind schedule but had cost more than we had planned.

The differences between these two explanations are important – not least to the ways in which we manage the future actions of our project. For if our future costs are likely to be less than the budgeted level, then we can use that difference. It can be used, for example, either to invest in additional resources – and thus complete the project earlier than planned – or to enhance the performance of the project by providing additional features. On the other hand, if our future costs look likely to exceed that budgeted level, then we need to make sure not only that we find out why that has happened but also that we control that cost over-run.

Earned Value

One of the ways in which we can solve this riddle – and find out what is actually happening – is to use the technique called Earned Value Analysis (EVA). This is used on many projects and has been refined and modified by the US Department of Defence into the Cost/Schedule Control System (C/SCS) for projects. C/SCS and EVA both attempt to show us what are the relationships between variances in cost and schedule and project performance.

Insight

EVA, when properly applied, has the unique ability to combine measurements of outcome, time and cost in a single integrated system and, in so doing, provide an early warning of performance problems.

Here's a simple example. Let's assume that we need to build a brick wall. As this is a large wall, we allow a period of 15 hours for its completion – including the time needed for the hand excavation and preparation of its foundation. The total budgeted labour cost is $80. But after 15 hours our monitoring tells us that all is not going well. There have been problems with the foundations. We find that $85 of direct labour costs has been billed and the job isn't complete. Only three-quarters of the bricks have been laid!

So, what can we find out from this and – more importantly – what can we do about it?

Earned Value Analysis (EVA) tells us that after 15 hours:

▶ **Budgeted Cost of Work Performed (BCWP)** – or **Earned Value (EV)** – *is equal to:*
(Units of work actually done × budgeted unit cost)
= $(0.75 × 80) or $(0.75 × 15 × 80/15) = $60.0

▶ **Actual Cost of Work Performed (ACWP)** – or **Actual Cost (AC)** – *is equal to:*
(Units of work actually done × actual unit cost)
= $85

▶ **Budgeted Cost of the Work Scheduled (BCWS)** – or **Planned Value (PV)** – *is equal to:*
(Units of work scheduled × budgeted unit cost) = $80

From these three figures we can work out:

Cost Variance (CV)

This is the difference between the **Earned Value** and the **Actual Cost** – or (**BCWP – ACWP**) – and is equal to:

($60 – $85) = a negative variance of $25 or 42% of the Earned Value.

A positive value for this variance represents a favourable position and a negative value, an unfavourable one.

Schedule Variance (SV)

This is the difference between the **Earned Value** of the work performed and the **Budgeted Value of the Work Planned** – or (**BCWP – BCWS**) – and is equal to:

($60 – $80) = a negative variance of $20 or 33% of the Earned Value.

A positive value for this variance represents a favourable position and a negative value, an unfavourable one.

These variances not only tell the project manager about the true, rather than the apparent, state of the project, they also give him or her pointers as to where actions will help to bring the costs of the project back under control. In this case, the larger Cost Variance and the fact that we know that there had been problems with digging the foundations tell us that we need to look at machine – rather than hand – excavation of foundations.

A simpler and easy-to-use variant of EV Analysis is the Critical Ratio. This ratio is made up of (Actual Progress/Scheduled Progress) × (Budgeted Cost/Actual Cost) and its value tells us whether we need to investigate further. For example, the value of the Critical Ratio for our wall would have been:

(0.75) × ($80/$85) = 0.705

When the value of this ratio falls below 1.0 this tells us that there is a need to investigate a below-par performance. A value of 1.0 indicates that all is well with our project and a value above 1.0 indicates a need to investigate an above-par performance. The further the ratio is away from 1.0, the more urgent the need to investigate.

Monitoring – reports and meetings

We have already seen that effective communication is vital to the success of the project.

Once our project is under way, most of this communication is about the what, how and why of the project's progress. One of the ways that we can keep people informed is by progress reports. These need to be issued regularly, though they can also be issued when a special event or problem warrants it. While their primary purpose is to report the general progress of the project to the client – the project's paymaster – they should also be available to other stakeholders. These reports are an important element in the communication patterns of the project. As such they have to be understandable, concise and based on facts. They are generally read by busy people, so brevity is also desirable. Supporting data, where required, should be nested in appendices. Routine progress reports – in the form of tables of figures, Gantt charts or AOA networks – should be presented with limited comment. These reports are often complementary to another method of reporting project progress – the project meeting.

Insight

Good project communication isn't always easy – but it is essential.

Project meetings are important. They are the major arena within which project stakeholders exert their influence. As such they possess a considerable potential for conflict and disagreement.

Because of this our project meetings must be conducted in ways that are clearly and effectively focused on the achievement of results and targets. Managing a project meeting that achieves these objectives represents a real skill on the part of the project manager.

But even this skill must have a backcloth against which it is acted out. For our project meeting this consists of: agendas – that state the business to be discussed; minutes – that briefly record what was decided and who is to do what; and briefing papers, such as project progress reports – that ensure the participants are well informed. These project meetings should be brief – no longer than one and a half hours – events from which participants emerge better informed about the project, having been involved in decisions on key project issues and with a better understanding of their own role in the project.

We've already noted that the exchange of factual information plays an important role in these meetings. It's a role that is further enhanced when participants feel able to exchange opinions, views and feelings about those facts. Achieving this means limiting the size of the project meeting – probably to a maximum of ten people – and chairing the meeting with skill and sensitivity. Indeed, the effectiveness with which the chairperson role is carried out can make or break the project meeting.

Effective chairpeople are concerned with the process of the meeting, rather than advocating or representing a particular viewpoint, line or policy. Chairing a project meeting in this way is often not easy for project managers, who are, after all, responsible for the successful completion of the project. But project managers rarely act in teams of one. Delegating the responsibility for presentation of a particular viewpoint to another member of the project team is often an effective way of presenting material – without compromising the project manager's impartiality. In the end, a project meeting is only as good as the people who attend. If the meeting is to be valuable and effective, then these people must be willing to engage in a constructive dialogue with each other. Given that, and an experienced and capable chairperson, the meetings of our project not only help the ways in which we monitor our projects, they also help us to keep the project on course – by controlling it.

Controlling

When we find that the activities of our project are not as they ought to be, then we need to do something about it.

These detours from our project plan and budget can be about any aspect of the three features or dimensions of our project – Time, Cost and Performance. The ways and means that we use to correct or limit their effects – to regulate them – can be just as various. We may need, for example, to recruit additional contract labour to correct schedule slippage or to reduce staffing levels to bring activities with potential early completion dates back in line. Unexpected technical problems may need to be solved by additional and unbudgeted R&D spend, or market fluctuations may bring an unexpected bonus of lower than estimated raw material prices.

But the actions that we take must have a single exclusive overarching objective – to bring our project back in line with its plan or its budget. These actions, by which we control our project, must act to reduce the difference between what is actually happening and our project plan or budget. The feedback loop that helps us to do this is shown in Figure 8.4 overleaf.

Insight

Project Control begins with your first project plan and ends with your post project appraisal. It's about cost, risk, outcome quality, communication, time, change and people.

We've already seen that we can use the project plan to help us choose what these actions are to be. It can help us identify the probable results of our 'what if we...?' proposals and test the

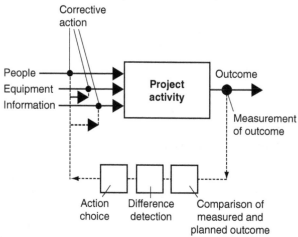

Figure 8.4 Feedback control.

feasibility of our options. In Chapter 2 we looked at some of the ways that help us to choose between one proposed project and another. These can also be used to help us choose between one possible action and another. The next chapter, Chapter 9, tells us about some of the ways that we can use to identify effective and economic solutions to the problems that can cause a project to drift 'off-course'. But, whatever we decide to do and however we arrive at that decision, our control of our project must have its roots in our monitoring. This lets us know when the activities of our project aren't as they ought to be. Then, and only then – when we have that information – are we able to act to correct or limit the effects of those variations from our project plan.

But these actions, if they are to be successful, must be distinctive in their style and nature. They need, for example, to be appropriate – to the project, its outcome and its stakeholders. They also need to be quick-acting – to ensure that the variation doesn't get out of control, and cost effective – to ensure that the cost of our control doesn't exceed its value. But, most of all, the actions by which we control our project need to be compatible with the variation's size and polarity. This means that there is no place in our project for sledgehammers to crack nuts or cups of water to douse infernos. The size or power of the actions that we take to control our projects must be appropriate to the size of the monitored departure from our plan or budget.

Getting this right can sometimes take real skill and judgement. There's never enough data to enable us to be absolutely sure. Our actions must be prompt and quick if they are to be effective. Whatever we do, we must also be sure that our actions generate results that oppose the forces that are driving our project 'off-course'. This means that while it's right to reduce expenditure in the face of a cost over-run, we also need to find out what the real cause of that over-run is. As we saw earlier in this chapter, Earned Value Analysis (EVA) can help here, as can some of the techniques we'll look at in Chapter 9.

But some of the differences identified by our monitoring will have causes that are too significant for the day-by-day remedial actions of our project control. These can range from the substantial, as when new technology becomes available, to the small, as when detailed design work progresses and shows us a better way to do something. Some of these will offer us the chance to do things in ways that are better than the ways we had planned. Others will have their roots in our mistakes and errors. Whatever their origin, nature or size might be, all of these significant changes have the potential to drive our project 'off-course' in terms of either its duration, cost or the nature and quality of its outcome. It is essential that we use our project change control procedure to control these modifications to our project. This, as we saw in Chapter 3, enables us to identify any changes from the project's 'base' line – as contained in the project specification – and then to evaluate, approve or reject those proposed changes at the earliest possible opportunity. Effective change procedures are an important tool in the way that we control our project.

Above all, the control that the project manager exerts must be:

▶ *based on facts, rather than on opinions*
▶ *targeted solely towards keeping the project in line with its planned duration, cost and outcome.*

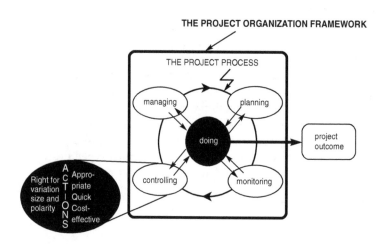

THE PROJECT ORGANIZATION FRAMEWORK

THE PROJECT PROCESS

managing

planning

doing

project outcome

controlling

monitoring

Right for variation size and polarity

ACTIONS

Appro-priate

Quick

Cost-effective

Figure 8.5 Controlling and the project process.

Take a look at Figure 8.5 and then use the following Checklist to check how good you are at monitoring and controlling your project.

How good are you at monitoring and controlling your project?

Under each of the headings below ring the number that is nearest to the way you feel you monitor and control your projects. Then add up your total and look at the Key comments.

1 Monitoring

I let things take their course.	1 2 3 4 5 6 7	I keep an eye on what's happening.
I measure everything.	1 2 3 4 5 6 7	I monitor the key aspects of the project.
I monitor the comple sophisticated aspects of the project.	1 2 3 4 5 6 7	I monitor easily understood, timely and relevant aspects.

2 Controlling

| These things usually sort themselves out. | 1 2 3 4 5 6 7 | I need to monitor what's happening and react in a relevant manner. |

| I react in the same way every time. | 1 2 3 4 5 6 7 | My reactions are geared to what's happening. |

Key

Total

5–15	You seem to be having problems.
15–25	Well done – use your low scores to identify where and how you need to monitor and control better.
25–35	You've either done it before – or aren't being honest.

What next?

The next chapter looks at the ways in which you can recognize, understand and, most importantly, solve your project's problems. But, before you do that, read through the following list – this chapter's ten most important messages.

TOP TEN MESSAGES

1 *Project monitoring is aimed at finding out where the project is in relation to its plan and budget.*

2 *Controlling a project is about making sure that project stays 'on-line'.*

3 *Project monitoring involves:*
    ▷ *measuring*
    ▷ *recording*
    ▷ *collating*
    ▷ *analysing data about the project.*

4 *Monitored data must be:*
    ▷ *relevant*
    ▷ *credible*
    ▷ *timely.*

5 *This monitored data must also be:*
    ▷ *understandable*
    ▷ *connected to the project plan and budget.*

6 *You can analyse this data by using:*
    ▷ *project milestones*
    ▷ *Limit Testing*
    ▷ *80–20 rule*
    ▷ *S curves.*

7 *You can also use Earned Value Analysis and Critical Ratios to get more information out of this data.*

8 *All of this information will enable you to decide what actions you're going to take to keep your project aligned with its plan and budget.*

9 *The actions that you take when you control your project must be:*
  ▷ *based on facts – rather than opinions*
  ▷ *targeted solely towards keeping the project in line with its planned duration, cost and outcome.*

10 *These project control actions must also be:*
  ▷ *appropriate to the variation they are correcting*
  ▷ *quick acting*
  ▷ *cost effective.*

9

Solving your project problems

In this chapter you will learn:
- *About techniques that can be used to recognize and understand project problems*
- *How to identify potential solutions to those problems*

Problems, problems and problems

In the last chapter we saw that monitoring tells us about our project's 'state of health'. Some days what it tells us is good: our project is 'on schedule', its Critical Ratio is close to 1.0 and its Cost and Schedule Variances are low. On other days, however, we are told that things are not as we desired or planned. When this happens we usually say that we have a 'problem'.

Problems and projects seem to go together like strawberries and cream or sausage and mash. Problems crop up, on almost a daily basis, in every project. These problems can be large or small and their consequences can be significant or trifling. But size and consequence aren't their only characteristics. For some of them come fully equipped with structure, certainty and a range of clear alternatives for their solution whereas others appear diffuse, uncertain, lacking structure and without solutions. In the folklore of project management most project problems are said to be caused by people and to have roots that reach back into the early days of the project (see Chapter 12).

But whatever their source, focus or nature, they all contain the seeds of potential upset and disruption for our project. For they all have the ability to cause delays or generate cost over-runs or to lead to shortfalls in outcome performance.

There can be little doubt about the fact that problem-solving is a key ability for the effective project manager. It is one of those 'must-have' skills whose presence makes a major contribution to project success; its absence can only lead to failure. As a would-be effective project manager, you can either become a problem-solver – or, alternatively, you can become a part of your project's problems.

A perfect world

In a perfect world, our project problems would arrive from our monitoring, neatly packaged and wrapped. They would contain all the data that we needed to define and understand them. Their arrival would be timely, giving us plenty of time to identify their best solution. We might even recognize them as problems that we had met – and solved – before.

Our approach to these paragons of problems would be logical and linear. First, we would review their symptoms. This would help us to identify or confirm their exact nature. Then we would generate a range of possible solutions – each complete with relevant data. Finally, we would carefully choose and implement one of these.

In the real world very few of our project problems are like this. Typically, they arrive with limited data, no structure and no clear alternatives. Their arrival often leaves us with little time to do anything other than to react. We rarely have enough information or enough time to be sure that we can identify, with absolute certainty, their nature. As a consequence we can seldom be sure that the solution that we choose is the best one. On some projects – such as development projects or high-risk, very innovative, projects – this sort of uncertainty is endemic.

But should we be surprised about all this? After all, our projects have, as we saw in Chapter 1, outcomes that are unique and it would be surprising if their problems didn't share that characteristic. Despite, or perhaps because of, this uncertainty, the first step towards solving our problems lies in defining them.

Frequency and consequence

How much definition do we need? Do we need to know all the facts, details, implications and subtleties of a problem before we can solve it, or can we cope with less than a complete picture?

Part of the answer to this question lies with:

▶ *how often the problem occurs*
▶ *what are the problem's potential consequences.*

For example, we need to know more about a recurring problem – because it keeps happening and, perhaps, because our previous attempts to solve it have failed. Infrequent or occasional problems appear to be less demanding in their data needs.

This can and does change when we look at the consequences of the problem. What we then begin to see is that infrequent problems with unacceptable – because of their cost or nature – consequences would demand and receive more attention; whereas low frequency problems with limited or acceptable consequence receive little attention. We saw this in Chapter 2 when we looked at whether we should reduce the risks associated with our possible future projects. For our problems, this marriage of frequency and the consequence is just as important. For it will give us – even if we have to estimate or guess both the consequence and the frequency – a basis on which to prioritize our response to a problem. If either of these is high then we need further data to define and solve the problem. If either of them is low then we can then either:

- ▶ *use the data we have to generate a solution*
- ▶ *defer solving the problem to a later time*
- ▶ *decide not to solve it until it either occurs more often or has greater consequences.*

The other part of the answer to the question, 'How much data do we need?' will often, in the 'real' world, lie in the answers to:

- ▶ *how much data do we have now?*
- ▶ *how much more data can we get and at what cost?*

The scope and outcomes of problem data-gathering must reflect:

- ▶ *the anticipated value of its outcomes*
- ▶ *the nature and accuracy of the input data.*

But, whatever the nature and scope of our data might be, we still need to solve our problems.

Logic or intuition

We don't always solve our problems in ways that are logical or rational. For example, we can 'jump' to a solution without evaluating any of the other possible solutions. Our choice of solution might be influenced by a number of factors such as personal preference and prejudice or the views of a strong leader or because this solution 'fits' with our long-term objectives. We can also arrive at a solution by intuition – without following any explicit or conscious logical train of thought. These and other similar processes are often referred to as 'creative' – rather than 'rational' – ways of solving our problems. They often seem unordered and complex. Nevertheless, they do represent powerful additions to the project manager's tool-box of problem-solving techniques. We shall look at some of them in the following sections of this chapter. However, none of us can afford to throw rationality to the wind and this chapter will also look at a limited selection of numerical techniques for problem identification and solution. For more problem-solving techniques look in the books listed in 'Taking it further' at the end of the book.

A nominal group

This method of solving problems uses a group of people to find potential solutions to an identified problem. A very productive technique that can generate lots of good high-quality ideas, it involves all the members of a group and uses consensus to evaluate and rank all the ideas generated. Its outcome is a group agreement about the action needed to solve a problem.

Insight
'Nominal' groups are more structured than 'brainstorming' groups and are thought to generate higher quality ideas.

The steps are:

Step 1 *The team leader presents the problem to the group. This must be done in a way that does not suggest a preferred solution. The process and ground rules are also explained at this stage.*

Step 2 *Working on their own, everyone writes down a list of potential solutions for the stated problem.*

Step 3 *Everyone, in turn, reports a single idea. This is recorded on a flip chart or board. The name of the person who suggested the idea is not recorded, nor are any comments or evaluations made. This continues until all the ideas have been recorded.*

Step 4 *During a brief discussion any clarification of ideas needed is given and similar ideas are amalgamated – but only if the owners of the original ideas are agreeable.*

Step 5 *Each group member then identifies what she or he thinks are the 'top five' ideas of this composite list. She or he writes these down on a piece of paper and gives this to the leader – without sharing it with the group.*

Step 6 *The leader generates a top five list for the group from these lists.*

Step 7 *This is reported to the group and then discussed. Another vote is taken to identify the idea(s) to be actioned.*

Most people find it difficult to report their ideas briefly and without commenting on their merits. The group leader must maintain the discipline of quickly moving on to the next person for each new idea. It is also important that the group stays together while the team leader – or someone else – is analysing the options to find the group's top five.

Force Field analysis

It was an American social scientist called Kurt Lewin who first expressed the view that the ways in which people behave can be represented as a balancing act. What we balance are the opposing forces that act upon us. In any situation there are a number of these forces – some of these will seek to promote a change in our behaviour and others will seek to restrain or limit that change. But this balancing act or equilibrium isn't fixed or frozen, it's a dynamic 'state-of-affairs' that interacts with the environment in which we work or play.

Insight

Driving or helping forces are typically positive, reasonable, logical, conscious and economic, while restraining or hindering forces are typically negative, emotional, illogical, unconscious and social/psychological.

If we want to change this equilibrium situation then we must either weaken one or all of the restraining forces or strengthen one or all of the forces for change. The resulting imbalance will mean that a shift or change occurs and a new equilibrium is established. The forces can be anything that acts upon or is relevant to the situation.

Force Field analysis can be used to solve our project problems. It is a simple, practical and proven way of deciding what you are going to do to solve your problem. You can use it on your own or in a team.

It has the following steps:

Step 1   *Identify the problem and the desired outcome.*
Step 2   *Identify the forces involved – it may help if you classify them as either 'helping' or 'hindering' towards achieving the desired outcome.*
Step 3   *Decide which are the strongest 'hindering' and 'helping' forces.*
Step 4   *Decide whether you are going to:*
    ▷ *increase the 'helping' force, or*
    ▷ *eliminate or reduce the 'hindering' force.*
Step 5   *Develop action plans for the above.*
Step 6   *Implement the plans.*

To work, this technique must have:

- ▶ *a clear and unambiguous identification of the problem and the desired outcome*
- ▶ *a detailed and comprehensive identification of the forces*
- ▶ *a practical and realistic implementation plan.*

This implementation can be seen as a sequence of three separate though connected stages:

- ▶ *unfreezing from current position*
- ▶ *moving to new position*
- ▶ *refreezing in new position.*

Each of these stages must be carried through to completion. For example, let's assume that we have decided to solve our problem of inaccurate or out-of-date data for activity work rates by changing from a manual system to a new project management information system (PMIS). The first – and unfreezing – step would be to choose the new system and then tell everyone that we are going to introduce this. The movement step would involve the commissioning of the PMIS. The last – and refreezing – step in this simple example would be to ensure that all future client records were completed and stored on the new system. If any one of these stages were not completed then the solution to our problem would not work.

The Ishikawa diagram

Diagramming can often help us to solve our problems. The Ishikawa, 'Fishbone' or 'cause and effect' diagram is one of the most powerful of the problem-solving diagramming techniques. Developed by Dr Kaoru Ishikawa, the diagram (see Figure 9.1) has, as its starting point, a box which is located on the right-hand side of a sheet of paper. The problem to be solved is written in this box and an arrow is then drawn across the sheet, pointing towards the box, and four further arrows are drawn pointing towards and joining the main arrow. Each of these side arrows represents a family or group of causes which could have led to the problem. In its purest form the Fishbone diagram labels these side arrows with the tags of the 5Ms: Machinery, Manpower, Methods, Materials and Maintenance. These can be extended to the 6Ms, by the addition of Mother Nature, or shrunk to the 4Ms by taking out Maintenance.

Insight

You should use an Ishikawa or Fishbone diagram when you:
- ▶ *need to find the root cause of a problem*
- ▶ *want to identify all the possible reasons for a problem*
- ▶ *need to identify areas for data collection.*

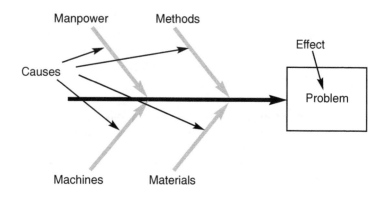

Figure 9.1 The Ishikawa or Fishbone diagram with 4M headings.

The technique can be used by a group or an individual and has the steps of:

Step 1 *Clearly define the problem.*

Step 2 *Identify all possible causes, by brainstorming or by using the early steps of nominal group technique to generate lists of causes rather than solutions.*

Step 3 *Group the causes generated under the 4, 5 or 6M headings.*

Step 4 *Visually connect all causes back to the problem using the Fishbone diagram. You may need to condense the cause descriptions at this stage.*

Step 5 *Use the diagram to continue the identification of possible causes until all of these, even the improbable ones, have been written down.*

Step 6 *Review the diagram and decide which of the causes are to be investigated first.*

Using the Ishikawa diagram results in a thorough and often penetrating identification of all the possible causes of the selected problem. It does not, of course, tell you which of those possible causes is the actual cause, but it does, if generated with care, give you confidence that all the possible causes have been listed. It is often worthwhile sticking to Ishikawa's original 5M headings in

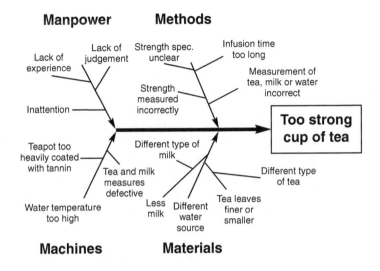

Figure 9.2 Example of the Fishbone diagram applied to a problem in the English Project.

order to make sure that the review of causes is comprehensive and methodical.

Figure 9.2 shows how the technique could be applied – using the 4M headings – to one of the problems of the English Project that we met in Chapter 4.

Pareto analysis

Most of our project problems have a range of possible causes. For example, our English Project tea can be too strong because the infusion time was too long or because the tea leaves were measured incorrectly or because we put in less milk than usual or because the tea leaves were old and dusty. If we have a repeated problem and if we've kept records of which of these causes seemed to apply, then we can use Pareto analysis to separate the major few from the many minor causes of our 'too strong' tea problem. Then we examine these major few further and develop action plans to eliminate them.

When Vilfredo Pareto studied the distribution of income in late 19th-century Italy, he found that around 80% of income went to about 20% of the population. He argued that this type of distribution is not just restricted to wealth or income but also occurs in many other situations. He then derived what is now called the Pareto principle. This tells us that, in general terms, the significant items in any group are in the minority – 'the vital few' – and the majority of the group are of relatively minor significance – 'the trivial many'. That is, that the minority of items in any group are the most significant in terms of their effect or consequences.

We can use Pareto analysis to identify the key causes of our project spend, as we saw in Chapter 8, and hence adjust our monitoring and reporting to reflect their importance. In our struggle to find solutions to our project problems, Pareto analysis can help us to identify those causes with either the highest frequency or the greatest consequence. In short, it enables us to focus our problem-solving efforts onto those key causes. As a result we should achieve maximum gain for minimum effort.

Insight

Pareto analysis not only shows you the most important problem to solve, it can also tell you how severe the problem is.

These are the steps:

Step 1 *Assemble your data. Since we are considering each cause relative to the others, absolute accuracy is not that important. What is important is that the data for all the causes has the same level of accuracy and that this level of accuracy enables you to discriminate between the individual effects of the causes. At this time you will need some idea about the factor that will be used to* contrast the effect of the individual items. This can be, for example, cost or frequency or consequence.

Step 2   Confirm that factor. It must be measurable but can also be generated by multiplying or adding or subtracting data for individual items. For example, the material usage costs can be generated by multiplying units used by unit cost. If it doesn't meet these criteria – then change it.

Step 3   Generate a table for the data in which you:
- ▷ arrange it in descending order, i.e. with the largest figure at the top
- ▷ generate the total for these figures
- ▷ calculate the individual percentages of that total for each cause
- ▷ calculate the cumulative percentage values.

Step 4   Identify those items whose cumulative percentage lies below the 80% level in the above table. These are the 'vital few' and can be shown graphically by plotting these cumulative percentages against the cumulative number or percentage of items or by generating a bar chart (Figure 9.3) for individual percentage of total cost. It is these significant items that you will subject to more detailed analysis or monitoring. The object of that further analysis and monitoring is to identify and eliminate the causes of problems.

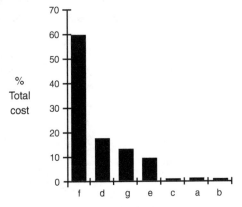

Figure 9.3 Bar chart of individual costs as percentage of total cost.

Pareto Analysis Example

Step 1

Item	Unit price (£ per unit)	Usage (000s)
a	30	2.67
b	12	4.18
c	450	0.2
d	75	20
e	1500	0.5
f	800	7.0
g	200	6.0

Step 2

Item	Cost (£)
a	80,100
b	50,160
c	90,000
d	1,500,000
e	750,000
f	5,600,000
g	1,200,000

Step 3

Item	Cost (£)	% of Total Cost	Cumulative % of Total Cost
f	5,600,000	60.41	60.41
d	1,500,000	16.18	76.59
g	1,200,000	12.94	89.54
e	750,000	8.09	97.63
c	90,000	0.97	98.60
a	80,100	0.86	99.46
b	50,160	0.54	100.00
Total:	9,270,260		

Figure 9.4 Pareto analysis example.

Figure 9.4 is an example of how we can apply Pareto analysis to the problem of project material cost over-run.

When we look at the Step 3 table and the bar chart in Figure 9.3 we can see that a minority of the items account for the majority of our project's total material spend.

That is:

▶ *items f and d account for 76.59% of this total*
▶ *items f, d and g account for 89.54% of this total.*

These items' contribution to project material costs is between seven and nine times greater than that of the remaining items. This means that if we reduce spending on these items it will have a major effect on the project's total material spend.

From this simple example we can see that by using Pareto analysis, the project manager can identify those items that make a significant contribution to the project's costs. We can also see that Pareto analysis can tell us what we need to monitor frequently and, as importantly, what we do not.

CUSUM technique

The cumulative sum or CUSUM technique is used to detect changes in the trends of measured data. It can be used, for example, to monitor the ways in which achieved labour costs change or the ways in which achieved outputs such as bricks laid per day, or wall area painted per hour, change. One of its strengths is its ability to detect early shifts or movements in the data monitored.

The technique involves comparing the measured data to a previously established target and then plotting the cumulative sum of the differences.

Insight

Using a CUSUM chart will enable you to pick up a small change faster and locate the time of the change more sharply.

The steps are:

Step 1   *Establish a target for monitored factor. This can be a desired value or an historic average.*

Step 2   *Subtract the first measured data from this target. The difference can be negative or positive.*

Step 3   *Use this difference to begin to generate the cumulative sum of these differences.*

Step 4   *Repeat Steps 2 and 3 for subsequent measured data and plot the value of the cumulative sum.*

A simple example is shown in Figures 9.5a and 9.5b in which we can see that the slope of the CUSUM plot changes when the measured value changes. It does this in a way which is not damped

Week no.	**Cable laid per day** (x 100m)	**Difference***	**Cumulative Sum of Differences**
1	6.2	– 0.2	– 0.2
2	6.7	+ 0.3	+ 0.1
3	6.9	+ 0.5	+ 0.6
4	5.9	– 0.5	+ 0.1
5	5.9	– 0.5	– 0.4
6	6.1	– 0.3	– 0.7
7	6.05	– 0.35	–1.05
8	6.2	– 0.2	–1.25

* Note: Target set at 640 metres per day

Figure 9.5a CUSUM example.

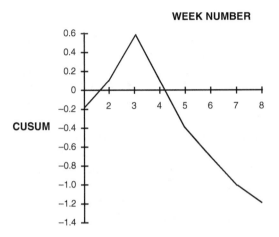

Figure 9.5b Graph plotting the value of the cumulative sum of differences recorded in Figure 9.5a.

by the 'smoothing' influence of any averaging process. This change tells us that something has happened and that 'something' may well require more detailed attention.

Multiple Cause Diagrams

Multiple Cause Diagrams aim to:

▶ *help you to sort out and refine your ideas*
▶ *identify cause and effect chains.*

Multiple Cause Diagrams are primarily about explaining why something has happened and the arrows in the diagram are used to indicate that one factor or event leads to or follows on from another. The steps for generating these diagrams are as follows:

Step 1 *Identify the outcome for which you want to establish the causes. and write this down on the bottom of your piece of paper.*

Step 2	*Identify the main factors that affect this outcome and write these on the paper above the outcome and linked to it by arrows.*
Step 3	*Identify the factors which affect those generated by Step 2 – write these above the Step 2 factors and link them to the Step 2 factors by arrows.*
Step 4	*Identify the factors which affect those generated by Step 3 – write these above the Step 3 factors and link them to those Step 3 factors by arrows.*
Step 5, etc.	*Continue as above until you have identified all the factors.*
Last step	*When you're sure you've identified and linked all the factors, then check your diagram over to make sure that it:*

> *does contain all the relevant factors, and*
> *has these in a correct relationship to each other.*

Insight

While each link on your Multiple Cause Diagram needs to have a logical cause and effect relationship, a single cause can have a number of effects.

Multiple Cause Diagrams are very powerful tools and can make a significant contribution to both the way your project team solves problems and the way it works together.

Here's an example:

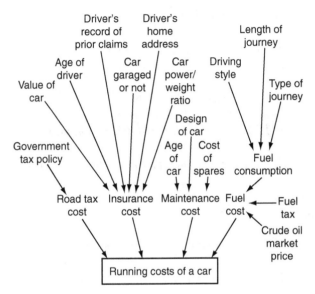

Figure 9.6 Multiple Cause Diagram.

What next?

Now you can look at what happens at the end of your project. In the next chapter you'll find out about how your project can be closed down. But, before you do that, read through the following list – this chapter's ten most important messages.

TOP TEN MESSAGES

1 *All projects have problems.*

2 *These problems can be large or small, or inconsequential or significant.*

3 *They can also be structured – rich in certainty and with clear alternative solutions, or lacking in structure – laden with uncertainty and without clear alternative solutions.*

4 *All problems have the potential to disrupt your project.*

5 *Solving project problems is a key ability for the effective project manager.*

6 *The first step towards solving a problem lies in defining it.*

7 *The amount of data that you gather for this definition must reflect:*
   ▷ *how often the problem occurs*
   ▷ *what its consequences are.*

8 *Problem solving can use a wide variety of techniques.*

9 *These include soft techniques such as:*
   ▷ *Nominal Group technique*
   ▷ *Force Field analysis*
   ▷ *Ishikawa diagramming*
   ▷ *Multiple Cause Diagrams.*

10 *They also include hard numerate techniques such as:*
   ▷ *Pareto analysis*
   ▷ *CUSUM analysis.*

10

Closing your project

In this chapter you will learn:
- *How to close down a project*
- *About the ways in which project closure can contribute to the success of both the closing project and the next project*

Endings

The end of our project usually arrives when the project outcome is formally handed over. We saw in Chapter 1 that this marks the transition from the Production phase into the Termination phase in the project's life cycle.

But not all of our projects have such clean cut and obvious endings. For example, when the boundary between the project organization and the client organization is blurred or diffuse – as often happens in the Integrated or the weak Matrix project organization (Chapter 3) – then the project outcome may not be the subject of a formal project team → client handover. It may have slipped gradually, almost imperceptibly, across the line between being a project outcome and becoming an organizational asset. When this happens the project outcome is gradually absorbed into the client organization as it grows and develops through the Production phase of its life cycle. Other projects collapse, fail or are terminated early. For these projects there is no project team → client handover to mark their end. They are abandoned. Their activity ceases, their failure becomes real. This, as you'll see in Chapter 12, can happen for a variety of reasons.

In all of these situations, whatever their point on the project
life cycle, the project's activities – its **doing** – stop. Despite this
apparent death, there is still work to be done, much of it about
the fine detail of the project. But the initial enthusiasm of the
project's early days has passed; project team staff will be looking
forward to returning to their pre-project duties or anticipating the
challenge of the next project. Nevertheless, this final stage of a
project still represents a challenge to the effective project manager.
In many ways, this challenge is greater than that of the earlier
stages of the project's life cycle. This 'end-of-the-project' work also,
surprisingly, possesses the potential to contribute to the success of
the project.

Closure and the project manager

We already know that a competent and effective project manager
must be able to lead, communicate, motivate and negotiate. In this,
the closing phase of the project, the demand for these skills is just
as high as it has been at any time of the project's life. The project
manager has, for example, to lead and motivate a project team that
is shrinking in size. The task of managing this shrinking team will
not be made any easier by the fact that individuals left in this team
may also be losing interest in the remaining tasks and showing
reduced levels of motivation. They may even be concerned about
their post-project futures.

The project manager also still faces the task of communicating with
the project's stakeholders. In the projects of our organizations the
client's senior managers will be showing less interest in the project.
Their attendance at project meetings will fall away, access to them

will become more difficult than it was in the project's early stages. The level of interest shown by the organization's operating staff will, however, be high. An all-consuming appetite for the details of the project outcome will have emerged.

In our homes, the project stakeholders will be just as involved or interested in the project outcome. The holiday in Hawaii will be in full swing, the sun-deck will have moved from pristine cleanliness to littered use, and the new car will have begun to lose that 'just-new' smell.

While all of this is happening, the business of project closure has to be carried out. The project manager will need, for example, to negotiate the completion of outstanding detail of the project outcome, contracts and work orders and the sale, disposal or storage of physical assets. She or he has to do so while the project team is shrinking and the stakeholders' acceptance of her or his authority is getting less. Small wonder then, that on large or complex projects, special project closure managers are appointed to ensure an orderly and effective end to the project.

But for all our projects – irrespective of their size, complexity or outcomes – all of these factors combine to create a unique and demanding set of problems which require management of a high order to ensure that the project is to be finally successful.

Insight

Project closure represents as much of a challenge for the project manager as the project start-up.

The closure process

When we close our projects we need to tidy up the loose ends. This means that we must ensure that all the project's work is done and its outcome is complete and available. It will mean that we need to make sure that all the projects records are complete, its contracts closed and its equipment is sold off, relocated or mothballed. The project team members will need to be reassigned and the project's surplus materials disposed of. In short, we need to close the project's books.

Insight

To be effective, the project closure process should ensure that a project is brought to a controlled end – rather than an out of control crash.

All of this must be planned and budgeted in the same way as any other phase of the project. Abrupt and unplanned closure doesn't just leave too many loose ends and information gaps, it also leaves the client and other stakeholders with an untidy mess that creates diminished confidence in both the project team and the project outcome. However, we need to recognize that the inputs and outputs of this closure process are different from those of the more active and 'doing' phases of the project – as we can see in Figure 10.1.

Earlier in this chapter we saw that the process of project closure can take place whether the project outcome is complete or not. We also saw that when closure is caused by project failure or early termination, there is no formal project team → client handover.

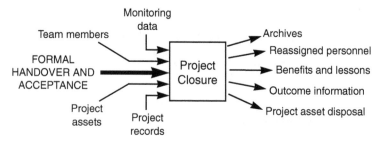

Figure 10.1 The project closure process.

But all the other elements of the project closure process remain. Project records need to be collated and stored, monitoring data archived, project assets disposed of or mothballed and team members relocated or reassigned.

If we fail to do all of this in an orderly and organized manner then not only do we leave behind the rubbish of our collapsed and incomplete intentions, but we also fail to learn from our mistakes and fail to grasp the benefits and lessons of managing our project.

Closing the team

Projects, as we saw at the end of Chapter 1, are about people. This was so at their beginnings and remains so through to their ends. Throughout the lives of these projects, these people *are* the projects. As clients or customers, as members of a club or a family, even as the proverbial man or woman on the street, they are involved and interested. As project team members, their creativity, adaptability and energy plot, plan and manage the project's course. In this, the final phase of these projects, the needs and concerns of these team members reach out beyond the now redundant boundaries of the projects.

In the project teams of our organizations they become concerned with the answers to such questions as 'When will I leave this project team?' or 'Which project will I work on next?' or even 'Will I get my old job back?' These remaining team members will have seen the composition and size of the team change as people – usually key experts – move on to new projects. They may even have seen the project manager depart, leaving the job of 'tidying up the details' to a project team member who is less experienced or may have occupied a junior role on the team. In the projects of our homes and families a tidy, organized closure of our project is overtaken by other events and so, inevitably, slips down the priority lists of our busy lives.

Insight
It's worth taking steps to ensure that the project team's
achievements are acknowledged.

All of this means that the ambitions and drive of the earlier, original, project team are gone. And with them, we may also have lost the co-operation and trust that carried the project to this, its completion. To manage this situation the project manager must make sure that both the project closure team and the client and other stakeholders refocus their earlier commitment to the project on to the task of project closure. The most effective way of doing this is by the use of joint teams; teams who are encouraged to self-manage the definition and implementation of the remaining project tasks. For example, joint project team/client/stakeholder snag listing teams can audit the project outcome and identify a jointly agreed list of outstanding work or defects. The project manager and the project outcome's primary user can create joint plans for its transfer.

But, in the end, the project team must break up. Like all break ups, this needs to be managed with care. It needs to take into account the needs of both team members and the project. The project needs to maintain, even until its last 'gasp', an effective project team. The individual team members need to have their achievements recognized in one way or another. Time spent, by the project manager, in planning this team wind-down – even to the point of involving members of our organization's project teams in the creation of a reassignment plan – will pay dividends in terms of the commitment and performance of the remaining team members.

Closing the project data banks

By the time we reach this, the final stage of the project:

- *almost all of the money will have been spent*
- *the project outcomes will have been created*
- *most of the project's resources will have been consumed.*

A considerable amount of information will also have been created.

The nature of this information is various. It can include, for example, such things as:

▶ *the drawings, technical specification and manuals of the equipment bought as part of the project*
▶ *the project outcome's technical or layout drawings*
▶ *the plans and programmes of project activities*
▶ *project spend records*
▶ *the contracts and subcontracts of the project.*

The baseline of this information was contained in the project specification, the project plan and the project budget. Their contents will have been modified and extended by the actualities of the project's activities and the modifications created by project change control procedure.

So what are we going to do with all this information? The answer is that we need to use it to:

▶ *identify and complete any outstanding work*
▶ *record the actual nature of the outcomes*
▶ *generate a project history*
▶ *check that we achieved what we set out to do.*

When these are complete – and not before – we will be able to say that our project is complete.

Activity completion

The first step that we make towards our project completion enables us to find out what, if anything, is left to be done.

In order to do this we need to find out:

▶ *what has been done*
▶ *what ought to have been done.*

> **Insight**
>
> Joint client/project team snag listing teams are an excellent way of making sure that everything is completed and that the client personnel get familiar with the project's outcome.

Not surprisingly, the difference between these will tell us if anything remains to be done.

Both of these have their roots and detail in documents such as the project specification, the project change control system and the Work Breakdown Schedule. With these as a starting point, joint project team/client/stakeholder snag listing teams can audit the project. They can physically check what has actually been achieved and then compare this with what should have been achieved. The differences, if any, that exist between these tell us what is left to be done, if anything. They might even tell us that we have done more than was needed!

Finding out what is left to do is, initially, the more important. The client stakeholder needs to be sure that the project outcome is what he or she intended when the project was given its go-ahead. When differences appear between the project specification and the actual outcome then the project manager needs to agree, with all concerned, a programme for completion of this outstanding work. This programme should have agreed priorities and time scales and an outcome that completes the project specification. Until that is achieved the project manager's attention cannot move on towards an orderly and well managed closure of the project. On large projects this closure process can almost be a project in itself and for that reason can, as we saw earlier in this chapter, be managed by a close down or termination manager.

In Chapter 5 we saw the importance of effective communication to the project. This, the final stage of our project, is no exception to that rule. Indeed, it can be argued that the unique pressures and difficulties of this stage increase the need for effective communication. For example, the joint project team/client/stakeholder snag listing teams will generate information and feedback about what they find. These will be used to agree completion targets and the work undertaken towards those targets will need to be monitored and reported. Communication is always a two-way process and the project manager and client or stakeholder decision makers will need to have access to each other in order to ensure that briefing and debriefing occurs and that this, the final stage of the project, moves to an orderly conclusion.

The ways and means of this communication already exist. They are the project meetings and reports that, as we saw in Chapter 8, have been a regular and routine feature of the project's monitoring and control systems. During project closure it may be necessary to hold these meetings more frequently and to allow them to consider matters of detail – such as snag list team activities or work outstanding. The composition of the meeting will also change – now including all of the members of the smaller project team and client or stakeholder personnel involved in snag listing, commissioning, etc.

Project outcomes

Included in the information that is created by the project is information that is particular to the project's outcome.

For projects with tangible outcomes there are drawings or technical specifications. Purchased equipment will have operating manuals and warranties. Prototypes will have development logs and performance records. Our holiday project will have copies of booking forms and brochures. Even when the project outcome is low in tangibility this information still exists – as in the publicity material of political campaigns or the completed questionnaires of opinion surveys.

Insight

Archiving this sort of information makes a major
contribution to the project closure process.

There should be little doubt about the need to transfer this material
to the client. For, in the future, it is the client, rather than the project
manager, who will need to refer to or upgrade this information. If
the project outcome is tangible, such as a new car or computer, it is
the client – rather than project personnel – who will be responsible
for its maintenance, repair or modification. Some of this information
will be needed immediately after the formal handover to ensure that
the client can start the operation and servicing of the project's
outcomes. On projects with large and complex outcomes the
handover of operating manuals may take place before the formal
project outcome handover, in order to ensure that the client can plan
and implement the training of operating personnel.

The collation and organization of all this documentation is not an
end-of-project event. As we saw in Chapter 3, this documentation
needs to be acquired, organized, collated and archived from
the earliest days of the project. For example, purchase orders
for equipment need to have clauses that ensure the provision of
operating manuals, maintenance schedules, spares lists and
trouble-shooting checklists. The delivery of this documentation
needs to be progressed and quality controlled in the same way as
the equipment itself.

There may also be circumstances in which the project team is
involved in the start-up of the project outcome. This will occur
when the outcome requires a particular expertise to ensure its
efficient and effective start-up and operation. This, typically, is
the sort of expertise that is difficult to acquire in any other than
hands-on operation. On projects with large and complex outcomes,
such as a chemical plant or an office block, the project start-up
team is usually a stand-alone team that comes into existence at the
late stages of the project's Production phase and may remain after
the rest of the project team has left. On projects with small or less
complex outcomes, such as a new personal computer or a car, the
formal handover will include a user familiarization session.

Project histories

All projects have histories. These have their roots embedded in the project's records. They tell us of the project's life and times, remind us of the twists and turns of the changes in the project's plan, confirm the who-did-what-and-when of the project and tell us which procedures and systems were used. They chronicle the life and times of the project.

On big, complex projects with extended time scales, the project history can provide a valuable insight to the ways and means of project management. It can also, if generated as a rolling history – rather than an end-of-project retrospective – serve as a useful induction document for new project staff. For most projects, however, the generation of a full project history is a luxury. Its inevitable cost or the limited nature of the project doesn't warrant its generation. Under these circumstances, our retrospective view of the project is limited to that of the audit.

Project audits

An audit can be conducted at any point in the project's life. Its objectives are simple and straightforward and aim to identify:

▶ *the project's current status*
▶ *the risks associated with that status*
▶ *whether we need to change the way the project is being managed or planned.*

It is, however, unusual for audits to be conducted in the doing phases – the Planning and Design and the Production phases – of the project. When this does happen, it is usually because of massive delays or overspends – factors which have caused anxiety and concern amongst the project's stakeholders.

However, when we conduct a post-project audit, the project actions and activities have been completed and the project outcomes have been handed over to the client. As a consequence the objectives of the post-project audit are to identify things like whether any cost or plan over-runs were justified and whether appropriate project management techniques were used. Obviously both the project manager and the client will have an interest in the outcomes of such an audit. Where both of these are employed by the same organization a single audit is not only sensible but also desirable. However, when the project manager/team is employed by a contractor then there may be value in an independent audit conducted by a third party.

The outcome of all post-project audits will be a formal report. The size, make-up and focus of this report will vary with the cost, nature and outcomes of the project. Large, expensive projects have audits which are conducted by a team of mixed disciplines and generate extended reports, usually to answer the needs of the organization's shareholders. The post-project audits of small or limited cost projects often consist of small reports. Reports on project outcomes with high levels of technical sophistication or those that require technical expertise – which the client may not possess – may be generated by independent technical experts.

However, these reports are not just book-keeping or cost accountancy exercises. They may, for example, reveal defects which are the subject of future legal action between a client, equipment suppliers or the project organization.

Post-project appraisals

Despite its investigative nature, the post-project audit does not tell us whether the project outcome has fulfilled its original promise and potential.

These, as we saw in Chapter 2, were an integral part of the information that we used to decide whether – or not – to spend the money required for the project's implementation. In Chapter 1 we saw that these outcomes can be concerned with any aspect of our lives – at work or at home. Their promises may have been about sales volumes and revenues, plant or equipment performance, reorganization, a new academic qualification, a new car or a holiday.

The post-project appraisal is about assessing whether what was promised was delivered and if not, why not. Without exception, it is initiated by the project client though it may be conducted, for reasons of impartiality or technical content, by a third party. In large organizations with many projects and high levels of capital expenditure, post-project appraisal is often conducted by a stand-alone department that is responsible to board level management. In our homes, our post-project appraisals are more informal in nature, often involving all who use or are involved in the project outcome. The post-project appraisals of the large projects of our organizations will review these projects from their conception through to two or three years after their completion. These reviews can take several months, involve a team of auditors and are presented in the form of a formal report.

As we saw earlier, the post-project appraisal is – whatever the size or nature of the project outcome – primarily concerned with whether the project outcome has fulfilled its original promise and potential. But it can also be used as a 'where did we get it wrong' and 'where did we get it right' sort of exercise. From it we may learn to estimate our costs or evaluate our risks in different ways or to use different sorts of project planning tools. These lessons can be about details – as in 'next time we'll hire a bigger holiday car' – or about more fundamental issues – such ass 'we'll never use that builder again'. All of these and other lessons come into being because of the post-project appraisal.

What next?

Now that you've closed your project, it's time to look at small projects and why they are different. This you'll do in the next chapter. But, before you do that, read through the following list – this chapter's ten most important messages.

TOP TEN MESSAGES

1 *Projects usually come to an end when they are formally handed over to a client stakeholder.*

2 *Projects can also come to an end when they are terminated or fail.*

3 *Closure of a completed project can, when undertaken effectively and efficiently, contribute to a project's success.*

4 *Project closure has the prime objective of the orderly and organized completion of the project.*

5 *This closure process also involves the transfer of project team members, the closure of the project's data banks and the completion of all the project activities.*

6 *Doing all of this and doing it well makes considerable demands upon the project manager.*

7 *A key part of the project closure process is the collation and archiving of all relevant documentation.*

8 *This project documentation can be about:*
   ▷ *the project*
   ▷ *the project outcome.*

9 *A project audit can be conducted at any point in the project's lifecycle and aims to identify:*
   ▷ *the project's status*
   ▷ *the risks associated with that status*
   ▷ *whether there is a need to change the way this project is being (or was) managed or planned.*

10 *A post-project appraisal is initiated by the project client and is about assessing whether what was promised was delivered and if not, why not.*

11

Small projects

In this chapter you will learn:
- *How small a small project is, or can be*
- *Why small projects are different*
- *How you can make sure that your small projects work*

Small, medium or large?

At the beginning of this book, in Chapter 1, we saw that projects can:

▶ *be large or small – or any size in between*
▶ *last for decades – or be completed in a day*
▶ *cost any amount of money – from tens to billions.*

We also saw that at the upper end of these bands of size, duration and cost we've got projects like the preparations for London's 2012 Summer Olympics.

London's 2012 Summer Olympics

Costing around £10bn, started in July 2005 and scheduled to be complete by August 2012, this project involves a complex mix of new build venues with existing and temporary facilities. These will cater for a total of 26 sports and include an 80,000-seat Olympic Stadium and the new Wembley Stadium. Most of these venues will be located in three zones within Greater London.

(Contd)

The proposed Olympic Village will have 17,320 beds, providing a comfortable and spacious environment with a wide variety of essential amenities for athletes. Public transport will undergo a massive redevelopment, including the expansion of the London Underground's East London Line, upgrades to the Docklands Light Railway and the North London Line, and the new 'Javelin' service.

But, as we've already seen, this sort of 'mega-project' is a rare event in most of our lives. For every working day, worldwide, millions and millions of projects with smaller outcomes, much more modest costs and shorter durations emerge, are planned, take place and are completed or fail. Some estimates go as far as putting the total world spend on these smaller projects at between 50 and 100 times the total spend on the mega-projects of the world. By the sheer weight of their numbers, these small projects are the significant majority of our projects and they crop up in almost every aspect of our lives.

But what, you might ask, do we mean by 'small'?

What is small?

When it comes to size, it is, of course, all relative.

For what is big to one organization is small to another. Similarly, what is costly to one organization may be inexpensive to another. For example, the World Bank, that mega-project funding agency, tells us that the small projects it supports in developing countries have a modest value of US$100,000. The US Government's multi-million dollar Federal Emergency Management Agency (FEMA) also tells us that, in 2007, the upper total cost limit for what it calls small projects was US$59,700. While the Massachusetts Institute of Technology (MIT) limits its small building projects to a total value of US$10,000, other sources tell us that a small industrial project will have a total cost of anything up to £3 million. Other views of what's large or small tell us that large projects need over 10,000,000 person hours while small projects require as little as 100 or less person hours. But cost or the person hours involved aren't the only things that we have to take into account as we approach a decision as to whether a project is small, medium or large.

Insight

Even on the smallest project there will be objectives that must be achieved.

There are further questions that need to be asked before we can take that decision. For example, we need to know if our project:

▶ *has an outcome that impacts on a single business unit or a limited number (<25) of end users*
▶ *stands clear of routine day-to-day operations or other projects*
▶ *has a cost that has a major impact on financial revenue*
▶ *can be staffed from existing personnel*
▶ *needs people from outside the organization – who may not be familiar with our business.*

When we think about these questions and our workplace we'll soon realize why they have to be asked.

For example, a project with a total cost of £100,000 would have quite an impact – in terms of its ability to be financed out of revenue – on an organization with an annual turnover of £1 million. Raise that turnover to £10 million and you've much less of a problem. Similarly, a project to replace a water filtration unit in a single low-capacity water bottling line would be more significant than the same project in a larger bottling plant that has three or four bottling lines. By now, you're probably beginning to realize that our judgement about the size of a project needs to take into account factors that go beyond the boundaries of the traditional project dimensions of cost, duration and outcome. For we also need to think about the *implications* of the project.

When these implications are substantial or significant, they must be taken into account. For example, a short-duration, low-cost project – like the replacement of an automatic filling and weighing machine in a small sweet or candy manufacturer's single production line – is one that has major implications for that organization. Such a project cannot just be called a small project. It may not be a mega or even a medium-sized project but it is, nevertheless, a *major* and *significant* small project for that organization.

The fact that a project outcome is significant can, and often does, make a difference to the way that we organize that project. For example, in the project above – for the replacement of an automatic filling and weighing machine – conventional criteria, as we saw in Chapter 3, tell us to use an Integrated project organization. But the implications – for the organization as a whole – of failing to complete the project on time would certainly include loss of output and might even result in cancelled product orders. Under these circumstances, the project organization adopted should be shifted to that of a Stand Alone project organization. In that sort of project organization, the skills and abilities of the filling and weighing machine supplier or manufacturer will be harnessed to ensure an on-time and working-well project outcome. All of this underlines what we saw in earlier chapters of this book. Namely that a project – whatever its outcome, duration or cost – exists within and interacts with the larger and enveloping environment of a business unit or organization. To be successful that project has to answer the needs of that business unit.

Small – a definition

Despite all of this diversity and disagreement we are, nevertheless, going to have to come to a decision about what is and isn't a small project before we go much further. We've already seen in Chapter 1 that dictionaries aren't much help when it comes to project management definitions. The *Oxford English Dictionary*, for example, tells us that 'small' means something that is 'of limited size; of comparatively restricted dimensions; not large in comparison with other things, esp. of the same kind'. But this definition doesn't go far enough – we need to generate a definition that's more specific and, if possible, takes into account the interaction between the project and the environment around it. So, from this point onwards, what we'll mean when we use the words 'small project' is a project that:

▶ *involves less than five people, often on a part-time basis*
▶ *has a duration of three months or less*
▶ *has a total cost of less than US$50,000 or £25,000*
▶ *is **not** significant in terms of the business operations of the client organization.*

This, of course, is about as basic as you can get in terms of small projects. But it is, nevertheless, the sort of small project that is commonplace in our homes and workplaces. It can also easily and quickly shift up a grade or two in importance – to become a major and/or significant small project. This happens when getting it finished by the planned time or to its planned cost becomes significant to, for example, our plans for next year's holiday, the remodelling of our homes or the expansion plans of our organization.

Let's move on now to take a look at what differences we'll find in a small project like this, and how we can make sure that this sort of small project is successful.

Differences

In earlier chapters we've looked at the ways that projects are:

▶ *chosen*
▶ *organized*
▶ *planned*
▶ *managed*

and the ways in which they:

- ► *choose and use their teams*
- ► *estimate and manage their money*
- ► *solve their problems*
- ► *are closed down.*

We will now look at what differences a small project brings to each of these aspects of the process of project management, but before we do so we need to be very clear that, when it comes to basics, we should manage a small project in just the same way that we manage a medium or large project. We should manage every project with the same level of professionalism and integrity. There is no room in small project management for 'back-of-the-envelope guesstimates' or 'making-it-up-as-you-go along' planning. Small projects need to be managed in ways that are just as professional, rigorous and effective as those that we would apply to a medium or large project. In other words – there is no room for amateurism, sloppiness or incompetence in small projects management.

Choosing a small project

In Chapter 2 we looked, in general terms, at what factors influence which project gets chosen from what is often a host of alternative projects competing for the limited capital available. When we trim our focus down to the small project 'market' you'll soon see that things get worse rather than better. This is because small projects thrive, flourish and proliferate. Almost all managers have a file full of – if not bulging with – little 'jobs' – or small projects awaiting the opportunity to get sanctioned. These 'jobs' are the ones that they would like to get done but can't afford to fund from their revenue budgets. Few of them are clear-cut 'must-do' jobs – in fact most of them are 'nice-to-do-when-we-can-afford-it' jobs. What all of this means is that you've got to be even more rigorous and particular when choosing which of your potential small projects you want to present to the boss or the capital sanction committee.

Risk analysis is a must – particularly if the project has outcomes that are significant. Doing this sort of analysis involves, as we saw in Chapter 2, a process that:

▶ *identifies the nature, source and likelihood of all foreseeable risks*
▶ *shows how that risk can be reduced or eliminated.*

Using numbers to support the case for your project is always worthwhile – providing you are clear and open about the accuracy of your estimates.

Organizing a small project

We saw in Chapter 3 that the Integrated project type of project organization usually fits best with small projects. This sort of structure enables us to:

▶ *use the project team members in a flexible part-time way*
▶ *tap into the resources and technical expertise of the larger parent organization.*

But it also blurs the boundary between the day-to-day responsibilities of project team members and the responsibilities implicit in their project roles. If this type of organization is going to succeed it must have a project manager who has:

▶ *the respect of the enveloping parent organization*
▶ *support from and access to a senior manager*
▶ *a clear, well-defined, remit.*

It must use the project procedures and documentation identified in Chapter 3 – particularly the Project Specification and Change Control procedures. But when you think about it, you'll soon realize that these conditions also apply when we shift – because of the significance of the project outcome – our small project organization over to the Stand Alone or even the Matrix type of organization.

Planning for the small project

Chapter 4 told us how important good planning is to the project. Effective planning is just as much a 'must' for small projects as it is for large or medium projects. You need to create your Work Breakdown Schedule (WBS) early and use it well to create your plan. Bar or Gantt charts, desktop computer produced or created and updated by hand, are particularly suited to small projects. Update your plan regularly and try to keep it simple – so that it can be used to communicate the 'what's happening' and 'what's due next' of your project to the rest of the organization. All of this may seem obvious but research tells us that around one in five small projects aren't planned – and that is a recipe for disaster!

Insight
Use project management software with caution.

Managing a small project

Managing any project and doing it well is a demanding and difficult task. For as we have already seen, in Chapter 4, a project manager has a role that is different from that of the day-to-day manager. For she or he has to:

▶ *use resources that are transient rather than fixed*
▶ *finish the project by a pre-specified and fixed point in time*
▶ *create a unique outcome.*

When it comes to small projects, these demands are doubled.

Why is this so?

To find the answer you need to return to our definition of a small project and remind yourself that on our small project all project staff – project manager included – often are part-time. This means that the project manager of a small project has to cope with the demands of her or his day-to-day role as well as the demands of her or his project management role.

Insight

Communicate accurately and often and when you do that focus on your project's schedule, costs, achievement and changes.

Doing this and doing well is far from easy. It requires the proverbial patience of Job and the ability to compartmentalize your thinking so that the problems and pressures of your day-to-day activities don't seep across the boundary into your project management role. But you're probably actually doing this already – when you cross the boundary between work and home. Try to remember, when you cross this boundary, that the management principles still are the same – it is just that the tools have changed.

Small projects and teams

When we looked at project teams earlier in this book (Chapter 6) we saw that a project team is a collection of people who come together for a defined and limited period of time in order to create a unique project outcome. Medium or large projects will be run by teams of six to eight people working full time on the project. Our small project team, however, will be different, for it will have a maximum of five people – all working on a part-time basis.

So, given that a good project team can make a significant contribution to the success of a project, do we have the makings of a team?

The answer is 'yes' – but only just.

There are two reasons for this. First, the fact that your project staff are part-time members of the team puts a significant strain on communications. It'll be all too easy to fall victim to the 'Oh, I thought you were going to do that' syndrome – a malaise that inevitably leads to project failure. Second, not spending enough time together as a team means that you miss out on that '2 + 2 = 5' phenomenon that gives good teams that extra spark of creativity.

Both of these have a simple cure – that of spending more time together. You don't have to have formal project meetings every time that you meet – but you do need to meet together regularly. Do that, and do it in a way that enables you all to keep up to speed with what is happening – both within and without the project. The smaller the number of people on your project, the more the need to overcome these difficulties by spending time together. But when you get down to the two/three people project staffing level, you'll really be pushing the limits in terms of being called a 'team'. Nevertheless, as you know from your own experience, it's still possible for small groups of people like this to do what teams do. That is they can:

▶ *make things happen*
▶ *work together in ways that outperform the sum of their individual efforts.*

Small projects and money

Money, as we saw in Chapter 7, is the life blood of a project. Underestimate your money needs or spend it profligately and you'll soon find yourself in a 'no-go' situation. Estimate well and manage your project money carefully and you'll find yourself moving steadily towards completion and coping well with the unknown or unplanned potential overruns that all projects experience. Small projects are no exception to all of this. Indeed, the fact that they involve less money than their larger cousins means that they are more vulnerable when it comes to cost over-runs. From the onset they are, as it were, nearer to financial wipe-out. But all of this doesn't mean that the small project's money is difficult to manage. On the contrary, the fact that small sums are involved makes small project management nearer to your own experience and gives you more confidence.

Make sure that your money systems are:

▶ *timely*
▶ *accurate*
▶ *compatible with and integrated into the systems of the larger organization.*

Get these right before you start – by talking to your organization's financial controller and asking for his or her help. Get them running well and your project budget will become a help rather than a hindrance.

Monitoring and controlling small projects

Money isn't the only part of your small project that we need to keep an eye on. As we saw earlier in Chapter 9, we need to:

▶ *find out where the project is in terms of activities, time and spend*
▶ *compare that to where the project budget and plan says that it ought to be*
▶ *take whatever actions are needed to keep the project in line with its planned duration, cost and outcome.*

The principles of project monitoring and control are just the same for small projects as those that are applied to medium or large projects.

Insight

Take corrective action promptly in order to head off the effects of adverse events.

The 'what' and 'when' of your monitoring should ensure that you know the facts – rather than opinions or hopes – about what has happened, is happening or is about to happen. You don't need tedious never-ending meetings or heavy-weight computer progress reports to get to these facts. Simple checklists or milestone reports – see Figure 8.2 – will be sufficient.

When these tell you there's a problem looming there are two things that you need to do:

▸ *make sure the project customer knows what is happening*
▸ *get your team together and focus on finding a solution.*

Small projects and problems

There are very, very, few – if any – projects that are problem-free. In Chapter 9, we saw some of the simple techniques that you and your fellow project team members can use to help to 'clear the fog' when it comes to problems and their solutions. These techniques are particularly suited to the solution of the small problems that you meet in small projects. Use these, use them well and use them often, and you'll find that they become an integral part of your project process. They'll also give you some good solutions to difficult problems.

Insight

Make sure that you get enough information to be able to recognize a problem.

Small project closure

Projects are transitory events and the small project is no exception. When this stage in the project's life cycle is reached you'll need, as we saw in Chapter 10, to make sure that:

▸ *all the planned activities and outcomes have been completed*
▸ *the project records and documentation are archived*
▸ *an audit of the project is undertaken.*

You'll also need to make sure that someone – usually the project client – has access to all the information that they need in order to conduct a post-project appraisal.

Insight

Don't forget to gather and file the project information.

In small projects, project records and documentation often suffer. Time is always limited and, as a result, decisions taken and data generated just don't get recorded. One way of overcoming this is for the project manager – or even the project team – to start and keep up a simple, handwritten, project diary. Using this to note down the 'what', 'why' and 'when' of the project – as or shortly after they happen – can make an immense difference to your project. Allow time for this when you plan your project. It's also worth remembering not to throw paperwork away during the earlier stages of the project. A simple, basic but well organized filing system can achieve wonders when the memory fails.

What next?

Projects fail all the time and in the next chapter you'll look at what failure means in the world of projects and, more importantly, find out what you can do to make sure that your project is a success. But, before you do that, read through the following list – this chapter's ten most important messages.

TOP TEN MESSAGES

1 *A typical small project:*
   ▷ *involves less than five people, often on a part-time basis*
   ▷ *has a duration of three months or less*
   ▷ *has a total cost of less than US$50,000 or £25,000.*

2 *Even small projects can have significant and major implications for the client organization.*

3 *Small projects must be managed in ways that are just as rigorous, effective and professional as larger projects.*

4 *Most small projects need to adopt an Integrated type organization.*

5 *Small projects need to use formal specifications, manuals, and procedures and keep accurate, well documented, records.*

6 *Small projects are usually best planned by using Gantt charts.*

7 *Managing and controlling project money and activities needs to be undertaken rigorously and effectively on small projects.*

8 *Communication is particularly important on small projects as most team members are part-time.*

9 *Effective problem solving is vital on small projects.*

10 *Small projects need to be closed as formally as medium or large projects.*

12

Project failure and success

In this chapter you will learn:
- **What project failure means**
- **How projects fail**
- **Why that happens**
- **What you can do to make sure that your project is a success**

Failure, and its counterpart, success, are common enough events in the workaday world of the 21st century. One – success – is desired, even lusted after, while the other – failure – is unwelcome, often feared. And yet, as we all know, you can't have one without the other. As Winston Churchill told us: 'Success consists of going from failure to failure without loss of enthusiasm.' This chapter will look first at project failure – its nature and causes – and then move on to use that information to establish what you need to do to make sure that your project is a success.

Insight

A part of the NASA Mars Surveyor Program, the Mars Climate Orbiter was to orbit Mars and collect environmental and weather data. But as the spacecraft approached its destination, telemetry signal fell silent and the $125 million project failed. The root cause of this failure was later identified by NASA to be the failure to convert data between metric and English units.

What do we mean by failure?

Failure is a word that we often use when something that we had wanted or planned to happen doesn't take place. Then there is, as the dictionary tells us, 'a failing to occur, be performed, or be produced'. When this comes to pass we describe the event or situation as a failure.

When you think about it you'll soon realize that, by and large, things fail quite a lot. Our buses, trains or aeroplanes regularly fail to arrive or leave on time; our bank, insurance and credit card companies repeatedly fail to provide the level of service that they had promised; and we come away disappointed from a movie that a friend had told us was 'great'.

Failures also happen in our projects. For example, a task that we had planned to finish by Tuesday doesn't get finished until Friday, or the cost of another task runs over our budgeted cost. As a result, our project has the potential to:

▶ *cost a lot more than it should*
▶ *take a lot longer than was planned*
▶ *have a product or outcome that doesn't do what it was supposed to.*

Insight

Success is the opposite of failure and is the result of thorough preparation and hard work as well as learning from previous failures.

Projects can also collapse and, as a result, be terminated early. For these projects there is no project team → client handover to mark their end. They are abandoned. Their activity ceases, their failure becomes real. This can happen for a variety of reasons. The project's planned outcomes, for example, may have become obsolete or been superseded by alternatives developed elsewhere. Cheaper or faster or improved versions of its outcome may have hit the marketplace. Its prototypes may have failed to reach their hoped-for performance levels. The project costs or schedule may have run out of control. Its senior executive project champion may have fallen by the corporate wayside. All of these and other reasons, as you'll see in more detail later in this chapter, can cause our projects to fail.

Nobody is happy when these sorts of things take place – none of us gets a medal and they're not what we wanted. But why do these sorts of things happen? For when problems first started to emerge, our project monitoring and control systems (see Chapter 8) should have told us what was happening and enabled us to do something about it.

In the early days of our project we should have:

▶ *evaluated the risk of these and other things happening (see Chapter 2)*
▶ *built additional 'float' or contingency time into our plan (see Chapter 4)*
▶ *added a contingency allowance to our project cost budget (see Chapter 7).*

Insight

Risk = (Probability of an event happening) × (Impact or consequences of that event)

Doing all of this should mean that we keep our project 'on track'.

Despite all of this, our project can still fail. To find out more about this we need to look at the 'how' and 'why' of project failure. Before we do that, we will take a look at the shape and size of success and failure in the world of projects. When we do that, we find that:

▶ *Successful projects:*
  ▷ *are completed on time and to budget*
  ▷ *have outcomes that are complete and as specified.*

- *Damaged or injured projects:*
  - *finish but overrun on cost and/or time*
  - *can also have incomplete outcomes.*
- *Failed projects:*
  - *are abandoned or cancelled*
  - *are incomplete*
  - *are written off as total loss.*

This tells us that project failure isn't limited to the black and white world of 'failed' or 'successful'. We can see that there are degrees of failure; degrees that range from partial failure – as in a damaged or injured project – through to total failure – as in a written-off project. We can use this view of failure as a base line from which we can look at why projects fail.

How and why projects fail

Project failures are expensive, frustrating, stressful events that can add an unwelcome twist to the cauldron of corporate politics as well as having the potential to damage your career. It is, therefore, worth trying to find out how and why these failures happen.

Insight

Failed projects aren't just about money. Project team members, managers, sponsors and other project stakeholders often work long hours trying to get a failing project back 'on track.'

However, it's not easy to find good project failure case studies. There are many reasons for this – including potential, actual or pending lawsuits, corporate reputations and, last but not least, embarrassment. Most of the project failure studies that are accessible have looked at failed information technology (IT) or management information system (MIS) projects. The picture that emerges is not a good one. Using the above definitions, it seems that, on average, in any ten typical projects:

- ▶ *only two or three will succeed*
- ▶ *a further four or five will finish damaged or injured in some way*
- ▶ *between two and three will completely fail.*

However, the literature of project management is rich in opinions about the whys and wherefores of damaged and failed projects. When you wade through these, a consensus does seem to emerge, one that tells us that the more significant causes of project damage and failure appear to be:

- ▶ *lack of user involvement*
- ▶ *inadequate or changing outcome specifications*
- ▶ *lack of senior management support*
- ▶ *inadequate or absent planning*
- ▶ *project management incompetence*
- ▶ *outcome is obsolete on completion*
- ▶ *inadequate or inefficient communication.*

It can be argued that some of these – such as project outcome obsolescence – are peculiar to IT projects. However, it is possible to find many of these causes in all sorts of project, for they shout out loud the presence of some very basic flaws in the project management process.

For in these failed or damaged projects:

- ▶ *project planning wasn't 'up to the job'*
- ▶ *project outcome specification wasn't defended*
- ▶ *clients or users weren't involved or communicated with.*

This view is confirmed when we look at the list of common causes of project failure produced by the UK Government's

National Audit Office. This tells us that most projects fail because of:

▶ *the absence of a clear link between the project and the client organization's key strategic priorities*
▶ *lack of clear senior management ownership and leadership*
▶ *lack of connection to and engagement with project stakeholders*
▶ *lack of project management and risk management skills*
▶ *project development and implementations stages not broken into manageable steps*
▶ *projects chosen on initial price or cost rather than long-term value for money*
▶ *supply side problems*
▶ *lack of integration between project team, stakeholder and suppliers.*

All of these have the potential to be found in your projects.

Insight

If you think that your project is heading for failure, then sort out your priorities by doing a 'triage' – and prioritize the sick or injured parts of your project for treatment according to the seriousness of their condition or 'injury'.

You have seen in earlier chapters of this book how important it is to make sure these and other key aspects of the project management process are undertaken effectively and efficiently. There are no short-cuts or bypasses on the road to project success. The key aspects of project management are so important we've devoted the whole of the next chapter to reviewing them. In the meantime, let's turn forward – towards project success.

Project success – the way forward

Now we know more about the what, why and how of project failure, we can begin to find out what we need to do to ensure our project finishes as a success. The literature of project management is also rich in views about how to do this. But before we look at those, remember that in Chapter 1 of this book we said that, if you are going to become an effective, creative, change-generating project manager, you'll have to:

▶ *need and want to be a project manager*
▶ *have or make the opportunity to explore being a project manager*
▶ *possess and use the knowledge needed to be a project manager.*

The first two are still down to you. But, by now, you should have enough knowledge to start or extend your project management career. To make sure that leads to success, what you need to do is to start with:

▶ *a clearly defined project specification*
▶ *a competent project manager and project team*
▶ *support from senior management*
▶ *sufficient resources (money, equipment, etc.)*
▶ *a planning system that you are comfortable with.*

Don't start until you have all of the above – you'll be wasting your time if you do!

But that isn't all that you need to do. For you also need to work hard and develop and use:

▶ *a team that works and solves problems together*
▶ *a plan that works and is responsive to change*
▶ *a communication system that reaches the right people*
▶ *a good, open and responsive relationship with client/user*
▶ *an effective change control system that defends the project specification you started with*
▶ *an efficient control and monitoring system that keeps you on course.*

When you get to a successful completion on your project you'll find that you have:

- ▶ *an outcome that's on time, within budgeted cost and meets the project specification*
- ▶ *a project history or audit that will help you, next time, to get it right first time.*

What next?

Now that you know what's needed for project success, it's time to review all that you've learnt about project management. That is what you'll do in the next chapter. But, before you do that, read through the following list – this chapter's ten most important messages.

TOP TEN MESSAGES

1 *Failure happens when something that we had wanted or planned to happen doesn't take place.*

2 *Successful projects:*
  ▷ *are completed on time and to budget*
  ▷ *have outcomes that are complete and as specified.*

3 *Damaged or injured projects:*
  ▷ *finish but overrun on cost and/or time*
  ▷ *can also have incomplete outcomes.*

4 *Failed projects:*
  ▷ *are abandoned or cancelled*
  ▷ *are incomplete*
  ▷ *are written off as total loss.*

5 *Projects fail or become damaged because of:*
  ▷ *lack of user involvement*
  ▷ *inadequate or changing outcome specifications.*

6 *Projects also fail or become damaged because of:*
  ▷ *lack of senior management support*
  ▷ *inadequate or absent planning*
  ▷ *project management incompetence.*

7 *Failed or damaged projects also suffer from:*
  ▷ *an outcome that's obsolete on completion*
  ▷ *inadequate or inefficient communication.*

8 *Projects will succeed when you start with:*
  ▷ *a clearly defined project specification*
  ▷ *a competent project manager and project team*
  ▷ *support from senior management*
  ▷ *sufficient resources (money, equipment, etc.)*
  ▷ *a planning system that you are comfortable with.*

9 *You'll also need to work hard and develop and use:*
  ▷ *a team that works and solves problems together*
  ▷ *a plan that works and is responsive to change*
  ▷ *a communication system that reaches the right people*
  ▷ *a good, open and responsive relationship with client/user*
  ▷ *an effective change control system that defends the project specification you started with*
  ▷ *an efficient control and monitoring system that keeps you on course.*

10 *If you do all of this when you get to the end you'll find that you have:*
  ▷ *an outcome that's on time, within budgeted cost and meets the project specification*
  ▷ *a project history or audit that will help you, next time, to get it right first time.*

13

....

Key issues for project management

In this chapter you will:
- *Read summaries of the key issues of project management*
- *Test yourself on what you've learnt*

This book has been a readable, practical and jargon-free introduction to the craft of project management. Its chapters have told you what is, and isn't, a project (Chapter 1), how to choose (Chapter 2), organize (Chapter 3), plan (Chapter 4), manage (Chapter 5) and monitor your project (Chapter 8), as well as how to assemble your project team (Chapter 6), manage your project money (Chapter 7), solve your projects problems (Chapter 9), close your project (Chapter 10), manage small projects (Chapter 11) and make sure that your project is a success (Chapter 12). Here are the key issues or Top Ten Messages of those chapters.

Projects, projects and projects
1 *A project is a way of creating change.*
2 *A project can:*
   ▷ *be large or small*
   ▷ *involve any number of people*
   ▷ *have a life span of days, years or decades*
   ▷ *have outcomes that are tangible or intangible.*
3 *A project has the act of doing at its core.*

4 This act of doing is supported and reinforced by the acts of:
  ▷ *managing*
  ▷ *planning*
  ▷ *monitoring*
  ▷ *controlling.*

5 A project is a one-off event that:
  ▷ *involves a sequence of connected activities*
  ▷ *takes place over a limited period of time*
  ▷ *is targeted to generate an outcome that is:*
    ▷ *unique, but*
    ▷ *well defined.*

6 A project's boundaries must be expressed in terms of:
  ▷ *time*
  ▷ *cost*
  ▷ *performance.*

7 Each of these must be defined at the beginning of the project and managed and controlled throughout its duration.

8 A project's life cycle has the phases of:
  ▷ *feasibility*
  ▷ *planning and design*
  ▷ *production*
  ▷ *termination.*

9 Each of these phases has its own different:
  ▷ *activity rate*
  ▷ *resource demands*
  ▷ *outcomes.*

10 All projects have stakeholders who need to be involved in the projects change process if it is to be successful.

Which project?

1 All projects involve risk and uncertainty.

2 Choosing a successful project means being able to identify the risks involved in that project.

3 You also need to identify the two Cs – causes and consequences – of those risks.

4 Success will follow if you identify the steps needed to reduce that risk and then take a rational, measured, decision whether or not to accept it.

5 *Some projects will arise because you need to react quickly to circumstances or when you don't have time to generate enough supporting information.*

6 *Projects like these are often responses to:*
  ▷ *the demands of a crisis*
  ▷ *the demands of legal requirements*
  ▷ *employee welfare needs*
  ▷ *an individual's power or status needs*
  ▷ *your organization's immediate competitive needs.*

7 *Some projects can just be 'nice to do' – such as a holiday.*

8 *The majority of projects are chosen by using numerical techniques. The simplest of these techniques are:*
  ▷ *relative ranking*
  ▷ *payback period.*

9 *The more sophisticated numerical techniques for choosing a project involve:*
  ▷ *Rate of Return*
  ▷ *Net Present Value*
  ▷ *Profitability Index*
  ▷ *Internal Rate of Return.*

Your project organization

1 *Projects need to be organized.*

2 *Choosing the sort of organization that your project will use is important.*

3 *That organization needs to be compatible with the client organization.*

4 *It also needs to provide a framework for the project's Doing, Planning, Monitoring and Controlling.*

5 *One alternative for your project organization is the Integrated organization which, as far as possible, is integrated into the line functions of the client organization.*

6 *Another alternative is the Stand Alone organization which stands completely free of and separate from the client organization, is self-contained and has its own resources, staff, premises, etc.*

7 *Matrix organization is a third and final alternative type of organization for your project that combines the good points of both the Stand Alone and the Integrated organizations.*

8 To choose the right organization for your project you need to:
  ▷ find out and understand what has worked in the past
  ▷ understand the client organization's skills, experience and equipment
  ▷ be aware of the project's outcomes, risks, costs, duration and special technology or knowledge needs
  ▷ decide what will work for you.

9 Then you need to generate:
  ▷ a project specification
  ▷ job descriptions
  ▷ responsibility charts.

10 You'll also need procedures for:
  ▷ budget control
  ▷ accounting
  ▷ change control.

Plans for your project

1 Your project plan enables you to convert the objectives of your project into concrete realities and outcomes.

2 To create that plan you need to know the:
  ▷ what
  ▷ when
  ▷ who
  ▷ with what
of the project's action.

3 You also need to know about your project's:
  ▷ budgeted cost
  ▷ level of outcome quality.

4 A Gantt chart gives you a picture of the project that is clear and easily understood.

5 An Activity on Arrow (AOA) network is an easily understood system of planning.

6 An Activity on Node (AON) network is well able to cope with change.

7 Small projects often use Gantt charts or AOA networks.

8 Large or complex projects usually use AOA or AON networks.

9 *The resource usage of your project can be planned and managed by using:*
   ▷ *resource smoothing*
   ▷ *heuristic rules.*
10 *Make sure that the project planning software package that you choose answers your needs.*

Managing your project

1 *Management is about organizing people and things so that they produce the results that you want.*
2 *This act of managing things and people happens quite a lot in organizations.*
3 *When you are a manager, you'll display leadership and authority and monitor and disseminate information.*
4 *You'll also take decisions, resolve conflicts and negotiate.*
5 *To become a manager you need to be selected, appointed and given formal authority.*
6 *Carrying out the role of manager will give you status and mean that you are able to access information and resources.*
7 *The role of project manager is different from the day-to-day operations manager.*
8 *The project manager.*
   ▷ *uses resources that are transient*
   ▷ *works to a time scale that is frozen*
   ▷ *creates a unique outcome*
   ▷ *is primarily concerned with the creation of change*
   ▷ *needs to be a gifted, broad-view generalist who can integrate or bring things together.*
9 *The project manager also needs to be able to:*
   ▷ *lead a team of skilled individuals*
   ▷ *communicate*
   ▷ *motivate the project team, contractors and sub-contractors*
   ▷ *negotiate effective solutions to the conflicts that arise in the project.*
10 *The effective project manager is key to the success of a project.*

Your project team

1 *A team is a social group – rarely more than ten people – who work cooperatively.*

2 *The people in this team will have shared objectives.*

3 *Good teams are about change – they make things happen.*

4 *They also work in ways that out-perform not only the sum of their member's individual efforts but also the efforts of all other sorts of social group.*

5 *You should have people in your team because of their functional skills and their ability to work co-operatively with others.*

6 *You should, however, also make sure that they are able to carry out the required team roles.*

7 *Building your team starts with the generation of a joint Team Charter and continues when the team spends time together and goes through the Forming, Storming, Norming and Performing stages.*

8 *Project teams are different; they consist of collections of people who come together for a defined and limited period of time in order to create a unique project outcome.*

9 *Project team members can be part or full time and will only be in that team for as long as their particular skills and knowledge are needed.*

10 *Successful project teams have members with:*
   ▷ *higher than average functional skills*
   ▷ *sensitivity to the 'politics' of both the project and its parent organization*
   ▷ *strong problem-solving skills*
   ▷ *a willingness to share both successes and mistakes – and then move on to the next target.*

Managing your project money

1 *A project's money starts with an estimate.*

2 *Creating an accurate estimate is vital to the success of your project.*

3 *A project estimate is based on the available information about the project outcome and the activities needed to achieve that outcome.*

4 *That estimate will also take into account the historic costs of identical or similar activities.*

5 *The types of estimate are:*
  ▷ *ball park, seat of the pants, order of magnitude estimate (± 50%)*
  ▷ *budget, predesign, feasibility estimate (±20%)*
  ▷ *sanction estimate (±10%)*
  ▷ *definitive estimate (±5 − 10%).*

6 *Top-down estimates use exponential or factorial estimating techniques.*

7 *Bottom-up estimates use costs generated from Work Breakdown Schedule (WBS) data by use of labour, material and equipment costs.*

8 *All estimates involve additional 'below-the-line' costs such as insurance and tax charges and allowances for inflation and contingencies.*

9 *An estimate becomes a budget when a project is sanctioned.*

10 *A project budget contains information about:*
  ▷ *how much money is to be spent*
  ▷ *on what that money is to be spent*
  ▷ *when it is to be spent.*

Monitoring and controlling your project

1 *Project monitoring is aimed at finding out where the project is in relation to its plan and budget.*

2 *Controlling a project is about making sure that project stays 'on-line'.*

3 *Project monitoring involves:*
  ▷ *measuring*
  ▷ *recording*
  ▷ *collating*
  ▷ *analysing data about the project.*

4 *Monitored data must be:*
  ▷ *relevant*
  ▷ *credible*
  ▷ *timely.*

5 *This monitored data must also be:*
  ▷ *understandable*
  ▷ *connected to the project plan and budget.*
6 *You can analyse this data by using:*
  ▷ *project milestones*
  ▷ *Limit Testing*
  ▷ *80–20 rule*
  ▷ *S curves.*
7 *You can also use Earned Value Analysis and Critical Ratios to get more information out of this data.*
8 *All of this information will enable you to decide what actions you're going to take to keep your project aligned with its plan and budget.*
9 *The actions that you take when you control your project must be:*
  ▷ *based on facts – rather than opinions*
  ▷ *targeted solely towards keeping the project in line with its planned duration, cost and outcome.*
10 *These project control actions must also be:*
  ▷ *appropriate to the variation they are correcting*
  ▷ *quick acting*
  ▷ *cost effective.*

Solving your project problems

1 *All projects have problems.*
2 *These problems can be large or small, or inconsequential or significant.*
3 *They can also be structured – rich in certainty and with clear alternative solutions, or lacking in structure – laden with uncertainty and without clear alternative solutions.*
4 *All problems have the potential to disrupt your project.*
5 *Solving project problems is a key ability for the effective project manager.*
6 *The first step towards solving a problem lies in defining it.*
7 *The amount of data that you gather for this definition must reflect:*
  ▷ *how often the problem occurs*
  ▷ *what its consequences are.*

8 *Problem solving can use a wide variety of techniques.*

9 *These include soft techniques such as:*
  ▷ *Nominal Group technique*
  ▷ *Force Field analysis*
  ▷ *Ishikawa diagramming*
  ▷ *Multiple Cause Diagrams.*

10 *They also include hard numerate techniques such as*
  ▷ *Pareto analysis*
  ▷ *CUSUM analysis.*

Closing your project

1 *Projects usually come to an end when they are formally handed over to a client stakeholder.*

2 *Projects can also come to an end when they are terminated or fail.*

3 *Closure of a completed project can, when undertaken effectively and efficiently, contribute to a project's success.*

4 *Project closure has the prime objective of the orderly and organized completion of the project.*

5 *This closure process also involves the transfer of project team members, the closure of the project's data banks and the completion of all the project activities.*

6 *Doing all of this and doing it well makes considerable demands upon the project manager.*

7 *A key part of the project closure process is the collation and archiving of all relevant documentation.*

8 *This project documentation can be about:*
  ▷ *the project*
  ▷ *the project outcome.*

9 *A project audit can be conducted at any point in the project's lifecycle and aims to identify:*
  ▷ *the project's status*
  ▷ *the risks associated with that status*
  ▷ *whether there is a need to change the way this project is being (or was) managed or planned.*

10 *A post-project appraisal is initiated by the project client and is about assessing whether what was promised was delivered and if not, why not.*

Small projects

1 *A typical small project:*
- ▷ *involves less than five people, often on a part-time basis*
- ▷ *has a duration of three months or less*
- ▷ *has a total cost of less than US$50,000 or 25,000.*

2 *Even small projects can have significant and major implications for the client organization.*

3 *Small projects must be managed in ways that are just as rigorous, effective and professional as larger projects.*

4 *Most small projects need to adopt an Integrated type organization.*

5 *Small projects need to use formal specifications, manuals, and procedures and keep accurate, well documented, records.*

6 *Small projects are usually best planned by using Gantt charts.*

7 *Managing and controlling project money and activities needs to be undertaken rigorously and effectively on small projects.*

8 *Communication is particularly important on small projects as most team members are part time.*

9 *Effective problem solving is vital on small projects.*

10 *Small projects need to be closed as formally as medium or large projects.*

Project failure and success

1 *Failure happens when something that we had wanted or planned to happen doesn't take place.*

2 *Successful projects:*
- ▷ *are completed on time and to budget*
- ▷ *have outcomes that are complete and as specified.*

3 *Damaged or injured projects:*
- ▷ *finish but overrun on cost and/or time*
- ▷ *can also have incomplete outcomes.*

4 *Failed projects:*
- ▷ *are abandoned or cancelled*
- ▷ *are incomplete*
- ▷ *are written off as total loss.*

5 *Projects fail or become damaged because of:*
- ▷ *lack of user involvement*
- ▷ *inadequate or changing outcome specifications.*

6 *Projects also fail or become damaged because of:*
  ▷ *lack of senior management support*
  ▷ *inadequate or absent planning*
  ▷ *project management incompetence.*
7 *Failed or damaged projects also suffer from:*
  ▷ *an outcome that's obsolete on completion*
  ▷ *inadequate or inefficient communication.*
8 *Projects will succeed when you start with:*
  ▷ *a clearly defined project specification*
  ▷ *a competent project manager and project team*
  ▷ *support from senior management*
  ▷ *sufficient resources (money, equipment, etc.)*
  ▷ *a planning system that you are comfortable with.*
9 *You'll also need to work hard and develop and use:*
  ▷ *a team that works and solves problems together*
  ▷ *a plan that works and is responsive to change*
  ▷ *a communication system that reaches the right people*
  ▷ *a good, open and responsive relationship with client/user*
  ▷ *an effective change control system that defends the project specification you started with*
  ▷ *an efficient control and monitoring system that keeps you on course.*
10 *If you do all of this when you get to the end you'll find that you have:*
  ▷ *an outcome that's on time, within budgeted cost and meets the project specification*
  ▷ *a project history or audit that will help you, next time, to get it right first time.*

Take a look at Figure 13.1 and try out your project management knowledge on Figure 13.2.

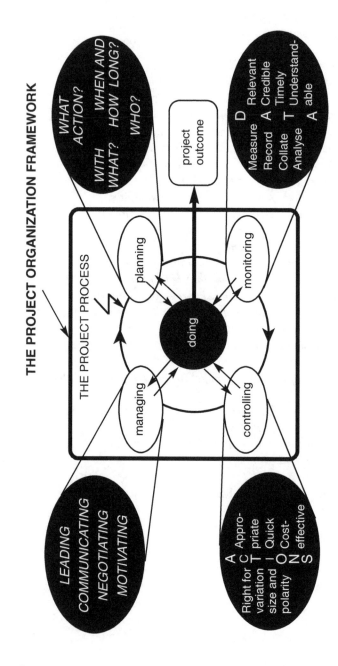

Figure 13.1 The project process — the whole picture.

Project Manager
Checklist

For each of the statements below, ring the number under the response which you feel is right for you when managing a project – and then add up your total.

	I agree	I agree most of the time	I'm not sure	I don't think I agree	No Way!
Monitoring is key to project success.	1	2	3	4	5
A project team can make or break a project.	1	2	3	4	5
If you listen to people, they listen to you.	1	2	3	4	5
Plans provide a strong basis for management decisions.	1	2	3	4	5
Change is an opportunity to be grasped.	1	2	3	4	5
Conflict can be good if managed well.	1	2	3	4	5

Key:

Total	
30–24	You can't be serious!
23–18	Some thought needed here.
17–12	Well done – a good score and a strong basis to build on.
12–6	Excellent – now go and do it.

Figure 13.2 Project manager checklist.

14

....

The changing face of project management

In this chapter you will learn:
- *How project management has changed over the decades*
- *How project management continues to change*

At the beginning of this book, you saw that the idea of the project – as a way of getting things done – has been around for a long time. You also saw that the more ancient of humankind's projects predate recorded history by a considerable margin – as in the earliest version of Stonehenge which is said to have been created in 3100 BCE. Nevertheless, despite all of this history and the billions of projects that have been started, created, failed or completed, it's only in the last hundred or so years that the idea of project management as a formal discipline – one that can be studied and taught – has emerged.

This process – the formalization of project management – seems to have started in the first decade of the 20th century. Around 1910, Henry Gantt, the creator of planning and control techniques such as the work breakdown structure (WBS) and resource allocation, introduced the bar or Gantt chart to the world. Soon phrases like 'project engineer' and 'project management' were in common usage. By the 1930s the Hoover Dam project in the USA was one of a group of major projects that brought detailed project planning, controlling, and coordination to the forefront. This project, which involved a spend of $175 million dollars, six different companies, a major worksite with no existing infrastructure, and approximately 5,200 workers, was brought in under budget and ahead of schedule. This process of change and development continued and, by the end of 1950s, the 'Program Evaluation and Review Technique' (PERT) and the 'Critical Path Method' (CPM) planning techniques had come into being and spread into use in many sectors of industry. In the late 1960s the International Project Management Association (IPMA) had been founded in Europe and the Project Management Institute (PMI) was founded in USA – both targeted to serve the interests of the project management industry. The introduction of the microprocessor in the early 1970s started a shift which took network planning from the mainframe to the mini computer and finally, in the 1990s, into our offices and homes with the desktop computer. In the 1980s the so called 'quality revolution' gave us the idea of Total Quality Management (TQM) and, for a brief while, the three dimensions of all projects (cost, time and performance) were joined by a fourth dimension – quality.

But these weren't the only changes.

For project management had to survive and serve in a world that was itself changing. Markets shifted from local to national to global; consumers rejected adequacy in favour of excellence, and the competitiveness and volatility of the market place spiraled upwards. In this hostile and demanding climate, our organizations had to learn to react quickly if they were going to answer the needs of their customers. The project began to be seen as a proven and effective way of doing that. It answered the strategic needs of the organization. As one project guru put it 'every project carried out for a commercial organization is a sub-project to that of achieving its corporate goals'. Projects like this enabled organizations to respond, effectively and efficiently, to those needs. In short, it enabled the organization to (as they say in TQM circles) 'delight' its customers.

But, in order to do that, the way that we managed our projects also had to change. This meant a gradual but increasing shift away from the essentially number-crunching, network-managing, resource-leveling style of project management. This took and continues to take us towards a style of project management which draws heavily on the so-called 'softer' people skills of negotiating, consensus seeking and communication. This is a shift that makes sense. It reflects the fact that, here in the first decade of the 21st century, projects are increasingly people-centric. They throw their net in an ever widening arc, drawing in stakeholders from far and wide – project team members, union members, government agencies, elected representatives, contractors, taxpayers, community members, environmentalists, political parties – the list continues to grow. It's a shift that also reflects the reality that managers, in general, are now more project-aware than they were in the past. For now, they, too, have access to sophisticated project planning software and can often use that software to effect, and their training has almost certainly included the basics of project management.

You can see the extreme leading edge of this shift more clearly when you read through the 'manifesto' of the Agile software movement – a movement dedicated to a new conceptual framework for undertaking software engineering projects.

Agile Manifesto

- ▶ Customer satisfaction by rapid, continuous delivery of useful software
- ▶ Working software is delivered frequently (weeks rather than months)
- ▶ Working software is the principal measure of progress
- ▶ Even late changes in requirements are welcomed
- ▶ Close, daily, cooperation between business people and developers
- ▶ Face-to-face conversation is the best form of communication
- ▶ Projects are built around motivated individuals, who should be trusted
- ▶ Continuous attention to technical excellence and good design
- ▶ Simplicity
- ▶ Self-organizing teams.

Nevertheless, managing a project continues to be a demanding task. But it's also a task that will continue to change and evolve. The purpose of this book has been to make success in managing a project more accessible for all of you, and to enable you to use the powerful change-creating mechanism of the project more effectively. The last section of this book – 'Taking it further' – aims to point you on your way to more advanced material on project management.

But in the end, the way that you manage your projects is up to you. It is truly an expression of your own individuality, rather than something brought down from some high mountain engraved on tablets of stone. My hope is that this book has enabled you to start to explore, change, refine and even, perhaps, reinvent the way you manage your projects.

15

....

Taking it further

_____

Books

Project management is a popular and growing topic, and there are always new books being published. This list is intended to start your further reading. To browse for (or buy) other books, try your local bookstore, The Bookstore on the PMI web site, or the Amazon, Blackwells or Borders web sites.

GENERAL

Cleland, D.I. (ed.), *Field Guide to Project Management*, 2nd edn, 2004, Wiley

Dinsmore, P. and Cabanis-Brewin J., *AMA Handbook of Project Management*, 2nd edn, 2006, AMACOM

Harvard Business School (ed.), *Managing Projects: Pocket Mentor Series*, 2006, Harvard Business School Press

Harvard Business School (ed.), *Managing Projects Large and Small*, 2004, Harvard Business School Press

Lock, D., *Project Management*, 9th edn, 2007, Gower

Meredith, J.R. and Mantel, S.J., *Project Management – A Managerial Approach*, 6th edn, 2005, Wiley

PMI, *Guide to Project Management Book of Knowledge*, 4th edn, 2009, Project Management Institute

Watson, M., *Managing Smaller Projects: A Practical Approach*, 2006, Multi-Media Publications

PROGRAMME MANAGEMENT

Reiss, G., *Programme Management Demystified*, 1996, Spon

Office of Government Commerce, *Managing Successful Programmes*, 2007, Stationery Office Books

PLANNING

Lewis, J.P., *Project Planning, Scheduling and Control*, 4th edn, 2006, McGraw-Hill

Lockyer, K.G. and Gordon, J., *Project Management and Project Network Techniques*, 7th edn, 2005, Prentice Hall

SECTORS

Brown, L. and Grundy, T., *Project Management for Pharmaceutical Industry*, 2004, Gower

Cotterell, M. and Hughes, R., *Software Project Management*, 2007, McGraw-Hill

Hughes, R., Ireland, R., Smith, N., Shepherd, D.I. and West, B. (eds), *Project Management for IT-related Projects*, 2004, British Computer Society

Martin, V., *Managing Projects in Health and Social Care*, 2002, Taylor and Francis

Melton, T., *Project Management Toolkit: The Basics for Project Success: Expert Skills for Success in Engineering, Technical, Process Industries*, 3rd edn, 2008, Butterworth-Heinemann

Ramroth, W., *Project Management for Design Professionals*, 2006, Kaplan Business

Schwalbe, K., *Information Technology Project Management*, 4th edn, 2007, Course Technology

ANALYTICAL METHODS

Chapman, C. and Ward, S., *Project Risk Management*, 2nd edn, 2003, Wiley

Fleming, Q.N. and Koppelman, J.M., *Earned Value Project Management*, 3rd edn, 2006, Project Management Institute

Swift, L. and Piffs, S., *Quantitative Methods for Business, Management and Finance*, 2nd edn, 2005, Palgrave Macmillan

COMMUNICATION

Baguley, P., *Instant Manager: Successful Workplace Communication*, 2009, Hodder

Conradi, M. and Hall, R., *That Presentation Sensation*, 2001, Financial Times/Prentice Hall

Harvard Business School (ed), *Running Meetings: Pocket Mentor Series*, 2006, Harvard Business School Press

Harvard Business School (ed), *Giving Presentations: Pocket Mentor Series*, 2006, Harvard Business School Press

ORGANIZATIONS

Morgan, G., *Imaginization: The Art of Creative Management*, 1997, Sage

Pedler, M., Burgoyne, J. and Boydell, T., *The Learning Company*, 2nd edn, 2007, McGraw-Hill

PROBLEM SOLVING

Adair, J., *Decision Making and Problem Solving Strategies*, 2007, Kogan Page

de Bono, E., *Six Thinking Hats*, 2nd edn, 2000, Penguin

de Bono, E., *Lateral Thinking – A Textbook of Creativity*, 1990, Penguin

Henry, J., *Creative Management and Development*, 3rd edn, 2006, Sage

Higgins, J.M., *101Creative Problem Solving Techniques*, 2nd edn, 2005, New Management Publishing Co

RISK MANAGEMENT

Chapman, C. and Ward, S., *Project Risk Management: Processes, Techniques and Insights*, 2nd edn, 2003, Wiley

Mulcahy, R., *Risk Management: Tricks of the Trade for Project Managers*, 2003, RMC Publications Inc

TEAMS

Belbin, M.R., *Management Teams*, 2nd edn, 2003, Butterworth-Heinemann

Belbin, M.R., *Team Roles at Work*, 1996, Butterworth-Heinemann

Cobb, A.T., *Leading Project Teams*, 2006, Sage

Katzenbach, J.R. and Smith, D.K., *The Wisdom of Teams*, 2007, McGraw-Hill

Journals

International Journal of Project Management – Elsevier Science Ltd, The Boulevard, Langford Lane, Kidlington, Oxford, OX5 1GB, UK

PM Network and *Project Management Journal* – Both at PMI Publishing, Four Campus Boulevard, Newtown Square, PA 19073, USA

Project Manager Today – Editorial Director, Unit 12, Moor Place Farm, Plough Lane, Bramshill, Hook, Hants, RG27 0RF, UK

PROJECTmagazine – www.projectmagazine.com

Professional associations

Australia
Australian Institute of Project Management
Level 9, 139 Macquarie St., Sydney, NSW 2000, Australia
Tel: +02 8288 8700
Fax: +02 8288 8711
www.aipm.com.au

France
AFITEP
17 Rue de Turbigo, 75002 Paris, France
Tel: + 01 55 80 70 60
Fax: + 01 55 80 70 69
www.afitep.fr

South Africa
Project Management South Africa
PO Box 1714, Halfway House 1685, South Africa
Tel: 011 315 0035

Fax: 011 315 2276
www.pmisa.co.za

Ireland
Institute of Project Management of Ireland
25 Upper Mount St., Dublin 2, Ireland
Tel: 01 661 4677
www.iol.ie/~instpmgm

Iceland
Project Management Association of Iceland
PO Box 8773, 128 Reykjavik, Iceland
www.vsf.is

United Kingdom
Association for Project Management
150 West Wycombe Road, High Wycombe, Bucks, HP12 3AE,
England
Tel: 0845 458 1944
Fax: + 44 014 94 52 89 37
www.apm.org.uk

APM is a founder member of the International Project
Management Association (IPMA), a federation of over 40 national
member associations.

United States
Project Management Institute
Four Campus Boulevard, Newtown Square, Pennsylvania, USA
Tel: +1 610 356 4600
Fax: +1 610 356 4647
www.pmi.org

PMI has 'chapters' in 45 countries including Australia,
Belgium, Canada, Chile, Egypt, France, Germany, India, Indonesia,
Israel, Italy, Japan, Luxembourg, Malaysia, Mexico, Netherlands,
New Zealand, Philippines, Russia, Saudi Arabia and
South Africa.

International
International Project Management Association
PO Box 1167, 3860, B D Nijkerk, The Netherlands
Tel: + 31 33 247 3430
Fax: + 31 33 246 0470
www.ipma.ch

IPMA has national associations in Austria, China, Czech Republic, Denmark, Egypt, Finland, France, Germany, Greece, Hungary, Iceland, India, Ireland, Italy, Republic of Macedonia, Netherlands, Norway, Portugal, Russia, Slovakia, Slovenia, Spain, Sweden, Switzerland, Ukraine, UK and Yugoslavia.

Project management qualifications

The idea that project management is a profession has been gaining increasing recognition for some time now. As a result, the number of project management qualifications that you can study for has also grown.

The qualifying bodies that validate these qualifications include:

- ▶ *The Association for Project Management (APM)*
  This UK based independent professional body
  (www.apm.org.uk) validates a number of qualifications
  ranging from an introductory certificate up to a Certificated
  Project Manager qualification.
- ▶ *Project Management Institute (PMI)*
  This American based not-for-profit association has a range
  of five professional certificates, the highest being that of the
  Project Management Professional (PMP)
- ▶ *Information Systems Examination Board (ISEB)*
  The Information Systems Examinations Board (ISEB) is a
  division of the British Computer Society (www.bcs.org) and
  validates three certificates in IS project management

▶ *National Vocational Qualifications (NVQ)*
There are several NVQ awarding bodies using the National Standard in Project Management and offering project management qualifications. These include Engineering and Construction Industry Training Board (www.ecitb.org.uk/) and Adexcel (www.edexcel.org.uk/)

The consensus seems to be that an APM validated qualification is best if you are working in the UK and Europe on non-IT industry projects, a PMI validated qualification if you are working for a US multinational and an ISEB validated qualification if you are in the IT industry.

Some useful web sites

Uncertainty – about access, stability and longevity – seems to be built into most web sites. In addition to those given above for the professional associations, here – in no particular order – are some other sites that are worth a visit:

evm.nasa.gov – NASA Earned Value page

www.acq.osd.mil/pm – Earned Value site with links and software tools pages

www.bsi.org.uk – British Standards Institution site. Check on BS 6079, BS 6046 and BS ISO 10006

www.prince2.org.uk – Official PRINCE2 web site

www.icoste.org – International Cost Engineering Council site. Link page to member associations

www.nssn.org – American National Standards Institution search site for international standards www.pmforum.org – Claims to 'Connect the World of Project Management'

www.atwebo.com/project_management.htm – Worth a visit for the links page

www.stason.org/TULARC/business/project-management-programs/index.html – A site which has some useful information on project management software

www.spottydog.u-net.com – UK consultancy web site with some useful guides

en.wikipedia.org/wiki/Project_management – Wikipedia's take on project management – interesting and useful

www.michaelgreer.com/links.htm – Michael Greer's page of project management links

www.astech-engineering.com/systems/avionics/aircraft/nasaprojectmanagement.html – 100 rules for NASA project managers

www.infinite.org.za/links1.htm – List of project management related web sites, including national associations for Austria, Denmark, India, Slovakia, Spain and Japan

www.wipmsig.org – Web site for women in project management – special interest group

www.pm4girls.elizabeth-harrin.com – Web site entitled 'A girl's guide to project management'

www.comp.glam.ac.uk/staff/dwfarthi/projman.htm – Dave Farthing's software project management links page

www.edwardtufte.com – The web site of Edward Tufte who has written several books on visual presentation of information

www.keirsey.com – Keirsey temperament sorter – useful for teams

www.teamtechnology.co.uk – MTR–i™ team roles site

www.tmsdi.co.uk – Margerison-McCann Team Management Systems Profiles home page

www.belbin.com – The Belbin team roles web site

Glossary

Activity An element of project work, usually has a duration, cost, and resource needs.

Activity on Arrow or AOA network A project planning method that uses arrows to represent activities – also called Arrow Diagram Method (ADM).

Activity on Node or AON network A project planning method that uses nodes or boxes to represent activities – also called Precedence Diagramming Method (PDM).

ACWP Actual cost of work performed. Also called Actual Cost (AC).

Arrow Diagramming Method (ADM) See Activity on Arrow.

Bar chart See Gantt chart.

BCWP Budgeted cost of work performed. Also called Earned Value (EV).

BCWS Budgeted cost of work scheduled. Also called Planned Value (PV).

Benefit-Cost Ratio See Profitability Index.

Budget A cost estimate for the project. The original cost estimate becomes the budget after sanction.

Cost Money given or surrendered in order to acquire, produce, accomplish, or maintain something; the price paid for something. (See also **Direct costs, Equipment costs, Fixed**

costs, Indirect costs, Labour cost, Material cost, Standard costs and Variable costs.)

Cost Variance Difference between the estimated and the actual costs. In Earned Value Management expressed as (BCWP – ACWP).

CPM Critical Path Method, a network analysis technique used to find project duration by finding sequence of zero or least float activities. Also called Critical Path Analysis (CPA).

Crashing Process of reducing project duration by analysing alternatives for duration reduction at minimum cost.

Critical Activity Activity with zero or negative float, any activity on the Critical Path.

Critical Path The sequence of activities which determines the earliest project completion.

Critical Ratio An Earned Value Management ratio: (Actual Progress/Scheduled Progress) × (Budgeted Cost/Actual Cost).

CUSUM Cumulative Sum technique, a technique for trend detection.

Dependency See Interdependency.

Direct costs Costs which can be specifically identified with an activity.

Discounted Cash Flow (DCF) See Net Present Value.

Dummy An activity in an AOA network which has zero duration but indicates interdependency.

Earned Value Analysis (EVA) A project performance measurement method which compares planned and scheduled work. (See also **ACWP, BCWP, BCWS, Cost Variance, Critical Ratio,** and **Schedule Variance.**)

EET Earliest Event Time, the earliest time by which an event can occur.

Equipment costs Cost of lease, purchase, hire and use of equipment used in project.

Estimate An approximate judgement, based on probability, of the cost or size of resources needed for a project task or activity.

Event The beginning or end of an activity.

Five Fundamentals All projects are one-time efforts, unique, about change and have limited and defined time spans, and defined outcomes.

Fixed costs Costs which remain at the same level irrespective of project workload.

Float The amount of time that an activity can be delayed without delaying the project completion.

Gantt chart A method of project planning. Activities are represented by horizontal bars whose length is proportional to the calendar time required for the activity.

Indirect costs Costs not associated with an activity but associated with common objectives.

Integrated project organization A type of project organization in which project activities are integrated into the structure of the client organization.

Interdependency When an activity cannot be started until a prior activity or activities are complete.

Internal Rate of Return The interest rate at which the project's Net Present Value is zero. (See Net Present Value.)

Labour cost Cost of employees.

LET Latest event time, the latest time by which an event can occur.

Material cost Cost of materials and other commodities.

Matrix organization A project organization in which the project manager shares control of and responsibility for team members with their functional boss.

Milestones Significant points in a project, usually events on the Critical Path.

Monitoring The acquisition, collation, analysis and reporting of data about project performance.

Net Present Value (NPV) The algebraic sum of the capital required to implement the project and the present values of the estimated future profits for defined number of years.

Node A point of connection in a project planning network, the beginning or end of an activity in an AOA network, the activity itself in an AON network.

Nominal Group technique Problem-solving technique.

Overheads See Indirect costs.

Parallel activities Activities which can be done at the same time.

Parametric estimating An estimating technique that uses historical cost data and relates it to outcome characteristics such as square footage, output, lines of software, etc.

Pareto principle A relationship that tells us that the significant items in any group are in the minority – 'the vital few' – and the majority of the group are of relatively minor significance – 'the trivial many'. That is that the minority of items in any group are the most significant in terms of their effect or consequences.

Payback period The period of time taken for the project's cumulative cash flow to reach zero.

PERT Programme Evaluation and Review Technique – a network analysis technique used to estimate project duration when there is uncertainty about activity durations.

Precedence Diagramming Method (PDM) See Activity on Node.

Profitability Index The ratio of the NPV of the project to the capital required.

Project A sequence of connected events that are conducted over a defined and limited period of time and are targeted towards generating a unique but well defined outcome.

Project key dimensions Cost, Time and Performance.

Project life cycle Feasibility, Planning and Design, Production, Termination.

Programme management The co-ordinated management of a portfolio of projects to achieve a set of business objectives.

Project specification The definitive source of information about a project's scope, goals and objectives, organization, budget and justification.

Ranking A method of choosing between alternative projects by generating the sum of each alternative's rankings, relative to each other, under a number of criteria.

....

Rate of return Annual profit/Implementation cost × 100%.

....

Resource Something that is needed in order to do work – money, equipment, people, information, skill, knowledge, materials.

....

Resource levelling Smoothing of resource usage patterns.

....

Risk The estimated degree of uncertainty.

....

Schedule Variance The difference between the scheduled and actual completion levels. In **Earned Value Management** expressed as (BCWP – BCWS).

....

Slack See **Float**.

....

Stakeholders People or organizations with something to gain or lose by the way the project turns out.

....

Stand-alone project organization A type of project organization in which the project team exists as a stand-alone organization – separate from the client organization.

....

Standard costs Calculated costs, often historic, which are used in both project estimating and monitoring.

....

Uncertainty The lack of information about the duration, occurrence or value of future events.

....

Variable costs Costs which vary with the rate of project workload or activity.

....

Variance The difference between what has been estimated or budgeted and what has been achieved. (See **Cost Variance** and **Schedule Variance**.)

....

Work Breakdown Schedule (WBS) A structured list of project activities and tasks with descending levels giving more detail.

....

Zero Float Condition which occurs when there is no excess or spare time between activities. (See **Critical Activity**.)

....

Index

CPSIA information can be obtained
at www.ICGtesting.com
Printed in the USA
LVHW03s1523280818
588394LV00010B/649/P